Francesco Arduini

The infant baptism

The case for a pandemic origin

In Memory Of
my dear friend Nevio
(1968-2021)

"Now he is not the God of the dead, but of the living,
for all are alive to him"
Gospel of Luke 20:38

Foreword

Petros Parthenis[1]

Most people love ready, clear-cut, authoritative answers – especially in subjects that do not really interest them. That's the case, even when they acknowledge that such information may greatly influence their lives.

History and religion are prime examples. For instance, in recent wars, people are ready to kill or get killed based on their conception of the past or of Christianity's or Islam's "genuine" teachings. Such grave decisions are often motivated by information given by "authorities". But how many of those involved have actually felt the need to verify personally what's a fact, an assumption, wishful thinking or downright fabrication behind the "truths" they have accepted? If there was a way to come up with a number, it would surely be a disappointingly low one. Amidst chaos, that warm sense of certainty emitted by such authoritative constructions of the past is the necessary drug that numbs the human conscience and facilitates cruelty.

In more peaceful times and areas, critical inquiry is much easier and more frequent, but still a minority hobby. Most people earnestly prefer to be told what "happened" in the past, who are their foes and friends, and what Jesus or Muhamad taught; and they readily accept it, especially if it agrees with what they already accept as true, thus boosting their confidence in their

---

[1] Petros Parthenis, Phd. on Ancient Greek & Roman History and Early Christianity.

belief system. Besides, life is too tiring and stressful to be filled with "unnecessary" inquiries and doubts.

Maybe that's precisely why researching and writing about the past is such a serious matter. And those few that undertake it should strive to present their findings without bias, even when their conclusions go against their own beliefs.

To be sure, that's not easy. It requires moral courage and strength; it's a challenge for anyone with an active conscience, and it becomes even greater when the subject under study somehow affects the researcher's personal religious beliefs.

It's like the work of an interrogator or a judge. Ruling and condemning is seldom a pleasant task and often takes an emotional toll on most jurists. But how much harder it would get when the accused is an old friend or a sibling? How agonising it would be if the defendant were the judge's father or mother? Still, the judge has to rule and make a decision based on facts - not suppositions, speculation or sentiment. Otherwise, he would have to resign from the case. He could possibly serve as an advocate of the defendants, or a legal advisor – but not as a judge.

Many scholars studying early Christianity feel a strong affection for their faith. And asking questions that cast doubts on that faith feels like accusing their father or mother of fraud. Hence, research itself can prove to be a stressful procedure. Several early Christianity researchers commence their study with the explicit intention of proving that their beliefs are the ones that genuinely reflect Jesus' teachings and the practice of his first followers. Unfortunately, few of them understand how damaging this stance can be to their purpose. A judge presisiding over his father's trial in order to prove his innocence will surely be disbarred and, consequently, cast even more suspicion of guilt upon his parent.

True enough, historians and judges are never purely objective. Modern historians have accepted that impossibility, and those conscientious enough always alert their readers before presenting their thesis to the general public. But, still, for interrogators and judges, nothing is (or should be) a priori certainty. Questions and uncertainty form the doorstep of both heresy and historical research. Hard questions need to be asked. Questions that could be seen as offensive when addressed to a loved one, thus risking the relationship with them. Similarly, Christians studying early Christianity have to ask questions that would surely sound irreverent to most of their fellow believers. "Reverence is a religious, and not a scholarly virtue," said B. Lincoln in his famous article "Theses on Method".[2] For the historian, there are no divinely inspired texts that simply cannot be wrong, no pieces of information that can't be touched by scrutiny. Who speaks here? What is the writer's intention and audience, and why? Is his testimony refuted or corroborated by other sources? Assessing from scratch every bid of information could easily cause a devout researcher to sense peril in this process. His pursuit of objectivity puts his relationship with his congregation –or even his creator- at risk.

That danger is not exaggerated. More than a few scholars started out as fervent believers in a doctrine and ended up rejecting their faith or some of their convictions. But if history is to be written, this risk has to be accepted.

Francesco Arduini has picked a subject that's undeniably of grave importance for billions of devout Christians around the world, himself included. Since Tertullian's famous apophthegm "that is truer which is prior"[3] –actually, even before that-, Christians thought that the best way to discover which tradition

---

[2] B. Lincoln, "Theses on method", *Method & Theory in the Study of Religion* 8.3 (1996), pp. 225-7.

[3] *Apol.* 19, 1: "auctoritatem litteris praestat antiquitas summa".

reflected Jesus' teachings most closely, was to identify the version that was older or attested earlier by authoritative Christian texts. Hence, tracing the origins of paedobaptism and determining when it became an established practice among Christians could affect the beliefs of numerous devout Christians practising (or rejecting) paedobaptism around the world. These are sensitive issues and should be treated as such. Still, the historian must state and justify his conclusions - respectfully, yet unhesitatingtly and clearly.

The origins of paedobaptism have been studied repeatedly by numerous scholars over the past century, several of which have been undeniably influenced by their personal beliefs. While a consensus hasn't been reached, most researchers consider paedobaptism a relatively late addition to Christianity – at least as an established and widely accepted practice.

Nonetheless, F. Arduini does more than revisit an already widely accepted conclusion. Accepting (justifiably) that the New Testament neither promotes nor documents paedobaptism, he examines methodically what the 2nd- and early 3rd-century Christian texts say (or don't say) about it. Next, he proposes a possible explanation for the numerous mentions of the practice that suddenly appear at the end of the second century and their stark contrast with the silence on the subject in earlier sources. The connection with the plague of the Antonines, an event that shocked the ancient world much more than we seem to understand, is intriguing and worth serious consideration.

The reader should be cautious to avoid the usual blunders afflicting the study of ancient texts – particularly early Christian writings.

Timespans between two writers and texts should be carefully weighed. Often, people seem to forget that 30 or 50 years were just as considerable and eventful back then as they are now. All texts should be examined within their social and historical milieu. A clear distinction should also be drawn between directives and actual practice. Most early Christian texts represent the ideas and teachings of prominent figures within a particular Christian community. Their opinion of what should or should not happen among Christians, while undeniably influential, should not be seen as what actually happened.

Regional and chronological diversity must be considered. Uniformity was never the case among Christian communities even before Paul's death, and 2nd century Christianity was much more diverse than it's often assumed. Even if something is proven as an established practice in a certain area or region, that does not necessarily mean that it was accepted as such by all or even the majority of Christians across the ancient world. Opinions that didn't survive past the 3rd or 4th century should not be instantly dismissed as minority or "heretical" features in early Christianity. Decades of research have shown that teachings rejected as "heretical" in later centuries were quite widespread or even dominant among Christians of the first three centuries AD –and vice versa.

Last but not least, the prevalence of a teaching or practice in 2nd-century Christianity cannot be judged merely by the number of references in the available sources. While indicative, it is undoubtedly not enough. Post-pacem Christians had no reason to copy texts that caused perplexity and embarrassment or could raise questions about the beliefs of eminent 2nd-century Christians that had been integrated into their tradition as pillars of their faith. This is probably why we have so few texts from celebrated figures of that period. We have a single letter from Polycarp, a true giant among 2nd-century Catholic Christians; almost nothing from any of Rome's bishops of that period. Justin is survived by three (or actually two) extensive treatises, but only through a single manuscript; if it had been lost, we would know almost nothing of his actual teachings. Indeed, 4th-century

Christians didn't seem too eager to copy their writings, despite venerating them as an invaluable part of their tradition. That is possibly because, judging from what little has survived from their writings, some of them, if not all, would be rejected as "heretics" if they lived two or three hundred years later.

Should historical, archaeological or other scientific research, conclusions or discoveries affect religious faith? Countless books and articles have examined the question, often in an effort to alleviate the anguish of devout believers that are startled by findings casting doubt on their convictions. Personally, I think that faith should always take into account scientific knowledge, even when if someone chooses, for any reason whatsoever, to stand firm in a belief questioned by research. Persons accepting paedobaptism should know whether the New Testament or 2nd-century Christian writings mention or promote this practice, even if such knowledge doesn't change their stance on the subject. Arduini's research will undoubtedly prove helpful in this regard.

Introduction

The dispute over paedobaptism

There has never been a Christian community that, at any time, has not requested baptism from those who wanted to be part of it since baptism has always been perceived and administered by the Church as an explicit commandment of Christ:

> "Go therefore and make disciples of all nations, baptizing them in the name of the Father and of the Son and of the Holy Spirit".[4]

Baptism marked (and still does) the concretely visible beginning of a life of fidelity to God. For the baptized, it is the binding confession of obedience, conversion, and hope in God through Jesus Christ. The importance of fully understanding all the facets of this commandment, which is the basis of the path of the Christian life, has always been considered fundamental by theologians and historians of Christianity.

The theological debate on the practice of baptism has been very heated in the past, especially during the 1950s and 1960s, particularly in relation to the legitimacy of imparting it to children and infants in particular. If today the tones of the debate have become somewhat muted, it is certainly not because a satisfactory conclusion has been reached but rather, to use the words of Gerhard Barth, due more to a certain "fatigue following

---

[4] Matthew 28:19. All biblical quotations are from New Revised Standard Version Updated Edition (NSREU) accessible at www.biblegateway.com.

the fervor of the discussion".[5] Accordingly, even though infant baptism has certainly become general practice today, recognized and followed almost[6] everywhere, the lack of *consensus* dictates that the discussion should still be considered open.

Violent "blows" to the practice of paedobaptism were inflicted by the theologian Karl Barth, according to whom there is no historical evidence that it was practised in the New Testament era or even later, at least not until the late second century. Barth's closure is total, both on the historical and theological fronts. He raises the following question:

> "How can the Church affirm today from many quarters [...] that she is and must return to being essentially missionary and adult, while, against all good knowledge and good conscience, she persists in dispensing water baptism with the same impudent prodigality that she has shown for centuries?"[7]

Barth is echoed by other important scholars. According to Kurt Aland, for example, the baptism of infants is not historically attested until the third century:

> "For the time before this [200 / 250 C.E.] we do not possess a single piece of information that gives concrete testimony to the existence of infant baptism".[8]

Holding the opposite view are a band of theologians whom,

---

[5] Gherard Barth, *Il battesimo in epoca protocristiana* (Brescia: Paideia, 1987), p. 11.

[6] Exceptions, for example, are Baptists and Jehovah's Witnesses.

[7] Karl Barth, *Il fondamento della vita cristiana* (Roma: Battista, 1976), p. 14.

[8] Kurt Aland, *Did the early church baptize infants?* (Oregon: Wipf and Stock, 2004) translated in English from the original *Die Säuglingstaufe im Neuen Testament und in der alten Kirche* (Gütersloher Verlagshaus, 1961), p. 101.

although few, believe there is clear New Testament evidence of infant baptism. Noteworthy among these is Oscar Cullmann, and according to him:

> "Those who argue about the biblical character of infant baptism must recognize the fact that adult baptism for sons and daughters born to Christian parents is even worse attested in the New Testament than infant baptism".[9]

And finally, there are those who espouse a third view on the whole issue, such as Alister McGrath, who says:

> "It is unclear whether the early church baptized children; the New Testament contains no specific reference to this. However, it does not explicitly impede practice, and there are a number of texts that can be interpreted as justifying it; for example, references to the baptism of entire families, including servants (who may have probably included children as well) on various occasions".[10]

Regarding the point that the New Testament "does not explicitly impede practice", one can easily understand how entire volumes could be filled with "things not explicitly said".

From such a silence, moreover, it would also be possible to deduce the opposite stance; that in the New Testament era the baptism of infants was utterly inconceivable. As for the baptism of entire "houses" or family communities mentioned in the New Testament and in which, at least according to some supporters of paedobaptism, there could also be infants, one cannot ignore the

---

[9] Oscar Cullmann, *Die Tauflehre des Neuen Testaments* (Zürich: Zwingli-Verlag, 1948), p. 21. (N.B. Whenever the translator's name does not appear, it is understood that the translations are made by me).
[10] Alister McGrath, *Teologia cristiana* (Torino: Claudiana, 2003), p. 515 ff.

fact that in these verses, the sequence of preaching-faith-baptism is always highlighted, which hardly applies to newborns. This argument, known as the "oikos formula", is to be understood as of very little evidential value because, as Gerhard Barth confirms, it has been amply demonstrated that "in the other New Testament passages in which we speak of 'NN and his house' children and in particular newborns are never included".[11]

---

[11] Gherard Barth, *Op. Cit.*, p. 175.

That a man should be baptized is, according to the Gospels[12], something that he owes to his free and conscious decision to recognize in Christ the figure of God by embracing His word of salvation. Christian baptism is the human work of the confession of fundamental faith that associates the Christian community with those who adhere to it. The New Testament writings clearly show us that a certain instruction in the Christian faith always precedes baptism in some way. To confirm this, in the Gospel of John we can read:

> "But to all who received him, who believed in his name,
> he gave power to become children of God, who were
> born, not of blood or of the will of the flesh or of the will
> of man, but of God".[13]

Those who are baptized become "children of God"[14], and Christ grants such only to those who have "received" him and to those who "believe"[15] in his name.

But how did we move from the documented New Testament situation to the current one? In the opinion of Karl Barth:

---

[12] βαπτίζω, the term associated with water baptism, appears 39 times in the Gospels. When the context allows us to focus attention on the baptized, we can always infer a conscious decision of the subject to undergo baptism. Analysis is based on the critical text of Nestle-Aland 28 (NA28), and it has been conducted through the software *BibleWorks*® vers.10: Matthew 3:6,11,13,14,16; 28:19 - Mark 1:4,5,8,9; 16:16 - Luke 3:7,12,16,21; 7:29,30; 12:50 - John 1:25,26,28,31,33; 3:22,23,26; 4:1,2; 10:40.

[13] John 1:12-13 (NSREU).

[14] Galatians 3:26-27.

[15] Mark 16:16.

> "In the bosom of the same church in full expansion, a baptismal practice began and spread according to which the original mutually receptive and spontaneous character of baptism, although still recognizable in certain substitute theological and liturgical constructions, *had nevertheless lost its meaning*".[16]

A "lost", or a bewilderment, of such gravity transpired that it led to the belief that infants should be baptized simply because they "physically" descended from "so-called Christian families" as if it were "a matter of affixing a mark".[17]

It seems correct to point out that, in my opinion, the argumentative balance and "serenity"[18] repeatedly requested by Barth to those who debate the question of paedobaptism lacked in his own exposition. In fact, no historical document exists that even suggests a baptism of infants practised within the Christian communities of the second century as a mere "physical" belonging.

---

[16] Karl Barth, *Op. Cit.*, p. 225 (italics added).
[17] *Ibid.*, p. 225.
[18] *Ibid.*, p. 232.

Ferguson argues that

> [w]hen we recall the high infant mortality rate of the
> ancient world, it is easy to understand how an emergency
> practice eventually became a normal practice. The early
> acquiescence in the emergency baptism of infants would
> account for the lack of controversy in the early church
> over the acceptance age for baptism.[19]

The fact is that today, the baptism of infants constitutes for
many an indisputable and untouchable dogma. In the Protestant
context, the Heidelberg Catechism states that:

> "[Children must also be baptized] ... because, just as they
> are understood like adults in God's Covenant and in his
> community, and to them, no less than to adults, are
> promised in the blood of Christ redemption from sins and
> the Holy Spirit who produces faith – so, through Baptism,
> a sign of the Covenant, they must be incorporated into the
> Christian Church and distinguished from the children of
> unbelievers; which took place in the Old Covenant by
> means of circumcision, in place of which, in the New
> Covenant, Baptism is instituted".[20]

Concerning Catholicism, the *Pastoralis actio* of the
Congregation for the Doctrine of the Faith of October 20, 1980,
states that the Church "has always held that children should not
be deprived of baptism" and that, for them, "this sacrament is
the entrance into the People of God and the door of personal

---

[19] Everett Ferguson, *Baptism in the Early Church: History, Theology, and
Liturgy in the First Five Centuries*, (Wm. B. Eerdmans Publishing, 2013), p.
401.
[20] Francesco Lo Bue, *Il catechismo di Heidelberg 1563*, (Torre Pellice:
Gioventù cristiana, 1939), pp. 49-50.

salvation".[21]

Many publications have been written to demonstrate not only the legitimacy and necessity of infant baptism but also that of this practice already existed in New Testament communities; just as many have been written to prove exactly the opposite.

It is not in my interest to contribute to the increase in the number of such publications by addressing in detail the individual verses of the New Testament that would or would not allow a glimpse of a baptism administered to newborns.

Nor do I have any interest in approaching the issue from a purely theological point of view. I find it much more interesting to examine the theme as described by the historical documents drawn up within the Christian communities of the second century.

The aim is to verify what the apostolic Fathers and apologists attested to regarding the baptism of infants, to highlight when this practice was unequivocally documented and, above all, to understand the reasons that led to increasingly clear positions in favour of paedobaptism.

I'll do that by introducing into the debate what is an original hypothesis of mine that could offer new useful insights to the discussion.

We will retrace the second century through the following works to arrive at the beginning of the third century, with the "Apostolic Tradition" and the now-attested practice of infant baptism:

Didache	ca. 100 C.E.
Letter of Barnabas	ca. 130 C.E.
Shepherd of Herma	ca. 140 C.E.
Apology of Aristides of Athens	ca. 140 C.E.

---

[21] DH 4670.

Apologies of Justin Martyr .... ca. 155 C.E.
Against heresies by Irenaeus .... ca. 180 C.E.
On Baptism by Tertullian .... ca. 200 C.E.
Apostolic Tradition .... ca. 215 C.E.

Chapter I

Didache

In 1873, Philotheus Bryennios, the metropolitan of Nicomedia, discovered in Constantinople a Greek codex written in 1056 C.E. (now preserved in the Patriarchal Library of Jerusalem) containing a work that, although its existence was known thanks to patristic mentions and quotations, was thought to have been lost. Following this discovery, ten years later, Bryennios published the first edition of the Didache: a text that brings together and elaborates pre-existing documents, probably composed by a Christian who had converted from Judaism. It is the very composition of the work that supports this hypothesis:

> "The influence of Judaism appears to you to be decisive, not only in the ethical field, in which the teachings of Judaism are accepted as they are, without any modification, but also in the liturgical field, as the Eucharistic prayers show".[22]

Having overcome the initial mistrust that tended to label the manuscript as a fake, there was then much discussion about the original date of composition without ever reaching a unanimous agreement. Jean-Paul Audet, a Canadian scholar who says that the work reflects the organization of the early Judeo-Christian communities and that it should be attributed to itinerant apostles, proposed a date between 50 and 70 C.E., but others are more

---

[22] Francesca Moscatelli, *Istruzioni per le comunità cristiane*, in: *Didaché: Dottrina dei Dodici Apostoli* (Cinisello Balsamo: Edizioni San Paolo, 1999), p. 24.

likely to date it towards the end of the first century[23], and still, others go back to the first decades of the second century[24].

The place of composition is doubtful: either Egypt or Syria have been proposed. In favour of the first, we have the languages in which the manuscripts were written (Alexandrian and Coptic); in favor of the second, we have above all, "the environment in which the Didache was written", namely "the important presence of Judaism [in Syria], abundant in our text".[25]

The structure of the Didache has three general sections. The first, known as "Two Ways", contains catechetical and moral information. The "way of life" is explained through a series of commandments to the negative, which refers to the Decalogue, followed by instructions of an exhortative and sapiential nature. As an example:

> "Thou shalt do no murder; thou shalt not commit adultery; thou shalt not commit sodomy; thou shalt not commit fornication; thou shalt not steal; thou shalt not use magic; thou shalt not use philtres; thou shalt not procure abortion, nor commit infanticide; "thou shalt not covet thy neighbour's goods"[26] (*Did.* II:2).

> "My child, flee from every evil man and from all like him. Be not proud, for pride leads to murder, nor jealous, nor contentious, nor passionate, for from all these murders are engendered"[27] (*Did.* III:1-2).

---

[23]Agostino Clerici, *Didaché. Lettere di Ignazio d'Antiochia. A Diogneto* (Milano: Ediz. Paoline, 2002), p. 13.

[24] Romani Penna, *Le origini del cristianesimo* (Roma: Ediz. Carocci, 2004), p. 218.

[25] Francesca Moscatelli, *Op. Cit.*, p. 24.

[26] http://www.earlychristianwritings.com/text/didache-lake.html.

[27] *Ibidem.*

Compared to the first chapters, the "way of death" set out in chapters V and VI appears much shorter. It begins as follows:

> "But the Way of Death is this: First of all, it is wicked and full of cursing, murders, adulteries, lusts, fornications, thefts, idolatries, witchcrafts, charms, robberies, false witness, hypocrisies, a double heart, fraud, pride, malice, stubbornness, covetousness, foul speech, jealousy, impudence, haughtiness, boastfulness"[28] (*Did.* V:1).

The second section[29] deals with baptism (Did. VII:1-4), where we read:

Περὶ δὲ τοῦ βαπτίσματος, οὕτω βαπτίσατε· ταῦτα πάντα πρειπόντες, βαπτίσατε εἰς τὸ ὄνομα τοῦ πατρὸς καὶ τοῦ υἱοῦ καὶ τοῦ ἁγίου πνεύματος ἐν ὕδατι ζῶντι. ἐὰν δὲ μὴ ἔχῃς ὕδωρ ζῶν, εἰς ἄλλο ὕδωρ βάπτισον· εἰ δ' οὐ δύνασαι ἐν ψυχρῷ, ἐν θερμῷ. ἐὰν δὲ ἀμφότερα μὴ ἔχῃς, ἔκχεον εἰς τὴν κεφαλὴν τρὶς ὕδωρ εἰς ὄνομα πατρὸς καὶ υἱοῦ καὶ ἁγίου πνεύματος. πρὸ δὲ τοῦ βαπτίσμος

Concerning baptism, baptise thus: Having first rehearsed all these things, "baptise, in the Name of the Father and of the Son and of the Holy Spirit," in running water; but if you have no running water, baptise in other water, and if you cannot in cold, then in warm. But if you have neither, pour water three times on the head "in the Name of the Father, Son and Holy Spirit." And before the baptism let the baptiser and him, who is to be baptized, fast, and any others who are able. And you shall bid him, who is to be baptized, to fast

---

[28] *Ibidem.*
[29] *Did.* VII-X.

προνηστευσάτω ὁ βαπτίζων καὶ ὁ βαπτιζόμενος καὶ εἴ τινες ἄλλοι δύναται· κελεύεις δὲ νηστεῦσαι τὸν βαπτιζόμενον πρὸ μιᾶς ἢ δύο[30].

one or two days before.[31]

The connection between the first and second sections is significant for our reasoning. The "precepts" that must be set forth "before", that is, before baptism, are those contained in the first section of the Didache. It seems evident that a certain work of catechesis was understood as a prerequisite for baptism. From the author's standpoint, this fact would tend to exclude a baptism of newborns, who obviously cannot be instructed according to the "way of life" or that "of death". It is also prescribed that both the baptizer and the baptized fast before baptism. This is also information that tends to exclude a baptism given to young children. A further reference to baptism can also be read in chapter IX:

μηδεὶς δὲ φαγέτω μηδὲ πιέτω ἀπὸ τῆς εὐχαριστίας ὑμῶν, ἀλλ' οἱ βαπτισθέντες εἰς ὄνομα κυρίου· καὶ γὰρ περὶ τούτου εἴρηκεν ὁ

But let none eat or drink of your Eucharist except those who have been baptised in the Lord's Name. Concerning this, the Lord said, "Do not give what is holy to the dogs".[33]

---

[30] Francesca Moscatelli, *Op. Cit.*, pp. 50, 52.
[31] Based on Lake Kirsopp's translation, amended by me. See footnote 26.
[33] See footnote 31.

κύριος· Μὴ δῶτε τὸ ἅγιον
τοῖς κυσί[32].

In this passage it is emphasized that baptism is, in turn, the prerequisite for participation in the Holy Supper. The Christian path, well defined, is therefore constituted by the succession: teaching-baptism-supper. Although these are the only points in which the subject is addressed, the Didache clearly testifies to us that, at the dawn of the second century, no form of paedobaptism seems to be foreseen.

[32] Francesca Moscatelli, *Op. Cit.*, p. 56.

The epistle of Barnabas, which has come down to us mainly thanks to the Sinaitic Codex of the fourth century and even earlier through fragmentary editions including a Latin translation (also partial) dating back to the second/third century, is a pseudoepigraphical writing, which critics have recognized as such since the end of the nineteenth century[34], elaborated by an unknown Judeo-Christian author. There are no explicit references to the place of origin and dating but, as Francesco Scorza Barcellona explains in his critical edition, to obtain such data, "we must rely on other elements that can be highlighted by a more in-depth analysis".[35]

The allegorical interpretation of Scripture that characterizes the whole epistle and that seems to echo the school of Philo, in addition to the fact that the first testimonies of this writing date back to Clement of Alexandria, have led some scholars to conclude that the writing came from the Alexandrian environment. But neither of these two points is to be considered decisive: Clement may have become aware of the epistle during one of the many journeys he undertook; as for exegesis, according to Scorza, "it is not properly pro-Philian or Alexandrian, except for chapter X".[36]

Other scholars agree that "the Alexandrian character of exegesis and the similarities with Philo have been exaggerated"

---

[34] To deepen the reasons, now outdated, of that criticism that identified the New Testament Barnabas as the true author of the epistle, I recommend: Samuel Sharpe, The *Epistle of Barnabas from the Sinaitic manuscript of the Bible* (London: Williams and Norgate, 1880).

[35] Francesco Scorza Barcellona, *Epistola di Barnaba* (Torino: Società Editrice Internazionale, 1975), p. 62.

[36] *Ibid.*, p. 62.

and that, in comparison, there are "more numerous points of contact with developments found in Palestine and Syria, for example in Qumran and rabbinic thought"[37].

In fact, it is impossible not to notice marked points of contact with other texts of Syriac origin. Also, according to Scorza, many passages are linked to the Ascension of Isaiah, the Gospel of Peter, the Syriac Apocalypse of Baruch and the Odes of Solomon.[38] If we add to this the fact that Syria is "also the seat of a particular type of Christianity linked to Jewish thought patterns even when it radically opposes Judaism"[39], we must conclude that the work was almost certainly written in a Syrian-Palestinian environment.

There has long been debate about the identification of the "kings" and "beasts" mentioned in Barn. IV: 3-5:

τὸ τέλειον σκάνδαλον ἤγγικεν, περὶ οὗ γέγραπται, ὡς Ἐνὼχ λέγει. Εἰς τοῦτο γὰρ ὁ δεσπότης συντέτμηκεν τοὺς καιροὺς καὶ τὰς ἡμέρας, ἵνα ταχύνῃ ὁ ἠγαπημένος αὐτοῦ καὶ ἐπὶ τὴν κληρονομίαν ἥξῃ, λέγει δὲ οὕτως καὶ ὁ προφήτης· Βασιλεῖαι δέκα ἐπὶ τῆς γῆς	The last offence is at hand, concerning which the scripture speaketh, as Enoch saith. For to this end, the Master hath cut the seasons and the days short, that His beloved might hasten and come to His inheritance. And the prophet also speaketh on this wise; Ten reigns shall reign upon the earth, and after them shall arise another king, who shall bring low three of the kings

---

[37] David T. Runia, Roberto Radice, *Filone di Alessandria nella prima letteratura cristiana* (Milano: Vita e Pensiero, 1999), p. 100.
[38] Francesco Scorza Barcellona, *Op. Cit.*, p. 62.
[39] *Ibid.*, 65.

βασιλεύσουσιν, καὶ ἐξαναστήσεται ὄπισθεν μικρὸς βασιλεύς, ὃς ταπεινώσει τρεῖς ὑφ' ἓν τῶν βασιλέων. ὁμοίως περὶ τοῦ αὐτοῦ λέγει Δανιήλ· Καὶ εἶδον τὸ τέταρτον θηρίον τὸ πονηρὸν καὶ ἰσχυρὸν καὶ χαλεπώτερον παρὰ πάντα τὰ θηρία τῆς θαλάσσης, καὶ ὡς ἐξ αὐτοῦ ἀνέτειλεν δέκα κέρατα, καὶ ὡς ἐταπείνωσεν ὑφ' ἓν τρία τῶν μεγάλων κεράτων.[40]

under one.
In like manner Daniel speaketh concerning the same; And I saw the forth beast to be wicked and strong and more intractable than all the beasts of the earth, and how there arose from him ten horns, and from these a little horn and excrescence, and how that it abased under one three of the great horns.[41]

If one could identify the Roman emperors to whom Barnabas alluded, one could also resolve the question of dating. Unfortunately, however, a unanimous opinion has never been reached in this regard.

Some scholars[42] have put forward the hypothesis that the epistle was written under Emperor Hadrian (117-138 C.E.). This hypothesis is based on Hadrian being in favor of the reconstruction of the Temple in Jerusalem and because Barnabas

---

[40] Francesco Scorza Barcellona, *Op. Cit.*, p. 84.

[41] Based on Joseph Barber Lightfoot's translation, amended by me. See http://www.earlychristianwritings.com/text/barnabas-lightfoot.html.

[42] Including Bart D. Ehrman, *Lost Scriptures, Books That Did Not Make It Into The New Testament* (New York: Oxford University Press, 2003), p. 219.

mentions the possibility of its effective reconstruction (*Barn.* 16:3-4). But these indications are entirely misleading because there is no evidence either to support the emperor's will to rebuild the Temple, or to support the fact that Barnabas was talking about the material, rather than "spiritual", reconstruction of the Temple of God. This does not mean that the time of writing cannot really coincide with this period, but simply that the evidence used to reach this conclusion, is inconsistent.

The only two elements on which unanimity exists are the *terminus ante quem* and the *terminus post quem*. The latter is to be fixed at 70-71 C.E. since Barnabas alludes to the destruction of the Temple, and the other is to be placed in the first decades of the second century, because of the links with the literature of that period and its extraneousness to the theme of Gnostic systems. Therefore "a dating between 95 and 130 CE"[43] is likely.

But how is this work structured? It could be schematized as follows:

      a) Introduction
      b) Anticultic debate
            a. The two peoples and the covenant
                i. Incarnation, passion, remission of sins
      c) Anticultic debate
                i. Baptism, passion, incarnation
            a. The two peoples and the covenant
      d) Anti-cultural debate
      e) Conclusion
      f) Two Ways
      g) Conclusion

The anti-cultural polemics and the strongly anti-Jewish character pervade the whole writing. The letter concludes with

---

[43] David T. Runia, Roberto Radice, *Cit.*, p. 100.

the treatise on the "two ways" which, together with the strong eschatological anxiety for the imminent triumph of the Kingdom of God, unites it with the Didache examined above. The purpose of this pseudo-Barnabas was to instruct his readers to achieve τελεία γνῶσις through the "appropriate" understanding of Scripture in typological terms.

The fact that this letter is at the end of the famous Sinaitic codex of the fourth century confirms the relevance it had for early Christianity. Although it was not included in the canon, its historical importance has undoubtedly remained unchanged to the point that some passages of this letter offer significant data for our research.

For example, concerning baptism, we can read:

> "We go down into the water laden with sins and filth, and rise up from it bearing fruit in the heart, resting our fear and hope on Jesus in the spirit."[44] (*Barn.* XI:11).

Baptism is therefore seen as a purifying action before the eyes of God. One immersed[45] oneself "full of sins" and acquired a status of divine approval.

But if paedobaptism had already been a recognized practice, this would be difficult to reconcile with another passage of the same letter, namely *Barn.* VI:11:

Ἐπεὶ οὖν ἀνακαινίσας ἡμᾶς ἐν τῇ ἀφέσει τῶν ἁμαρτιῶν ἐποίησεν ἡμᾶς ἄλλον τύπον, ὡς παιδίον ἔχειν τὴν ψυχήν, ὡς ἂν δὴ	Forasmuch then as He renewed us in the remission of sins, He made us

---

[44] See footnote 41.

[45] As also attested by the Didache, baptism by sprinkling was practiced only in *extrema ratio*. Most of the time they proceeded to baptize by immersion.

ἀναπλάσσοντος αὐτοῦ ἡμᾶς.[46]	a new type, so that we should have the soul of children, as if He was recreating us. [47]

Even in the account of the "heifer"[48], children are associated with a concept of approval from the Lord.

If the practice of baptism of newborns had already been in place, then both the "soul of the child" and that of the baptized would both be in a state of "purity", and therefore any comparison between the two would seem entirely superfluous. If, on the other hand, the neonatal condition of the child was considered pure regardless of the baptismal state, then the comparison of Barnabas would seem to acquire greater meaning and this would also give meaning to the subsequent statement according to which the newly baptized are to be considered as "created again" or reborn, in the same way as a newborn child.

These passages seem to confirm the idea that, for early Christianity, children (especially infants) already enjoyed divine approval regardless of their baptismal status.

A similar interpretation of Barnabas' thought is confirmed, perhaps even more clearly, by the examination of the later *Shepherd of Hermas*.

---

[46] Francesco Scorza Barcellona, *Op. Cit.*, p. 92.
[47] See footnote 41.
[48] Francesco Scorza Barcellona, *Op. Cit.*, p. 99.

Shepherd of Hermas

According to critics, the Shepherd is a work composed in the Roman environment in the middle of the second century. The author says his name is Hermas. The Muratorian Fragment[49] offers some useful clues for dating:

> "Hermas wrote the Shepherd most recently in our own times in the city of Rome, while the bishop Pius, his brother, was seated on the throne of the church of the city of Rome [...] And therefore it [the Shepherd] ought indeed to be read; but it cannot be read publicly in the Church to the people either among the prophets, *whose number is settled*, or among the apostles to the end of time".[50]

If the mentioned bishop was Pius I, then Hermas had to write his work shortly after 140 C.E.[51]; the fact that the communities of the second century urged it to be read, regardless of not considering it on a par with the other "inspired" writings, is an indication of the considerable importance that was attached to it.

The Shepherd is divided into three parts (five Visions, twelve Precepts and ten Similitudes). The whole work, except for the part of the Precepts, is a succession of visions and seeking to

---

[49] It is part of a manuscript codex consisting in 76 sheets of parchment 27x17 cm each. It was discovered by Ludovico Antonio Muratori in the Biblioteca Ambrosiana in Milan and published in 1740. It seems that the codex was produced in the eighth century in the ancient monastery of Bobbio, near Piacenza, and then transferred to the Ambrosiana Library in the early seventeenth century.

[50] Geoffrey Mark Hahneman, *The Muratorian Fragment and the Development of the Canon* (Oxford: Oxford University Press, 1992), p. 43, 202.

[51] DH 105.

understand their meaning, Hermas asks his guides a series of questions. The problem of the remission of post-baptismal sins is addressed. To fully grasp the gravity of this problem, one must understand the social framework surrounding Christianity at that time. According to Ernesto Buonaiuti:

> "The picture that the Pastor of Hermas presents to us of the Christian society of the time is not really the most attractive. Bishops, priests, deacons and faithful depart scandalously from the path of duty and put earthly interests before the sacred interests of the spirit. Hence the problem that the author proposes with trembling hesitation. These believers and refugees, who have already received baptism, what chance do they have of obtaining the remission of their sins, salvation?".[52]

It was generally believed that sins were forgiven only with baptism, but the considerable increase in believers[53] and serious sins committed required a solution that avoided, or at least limited, the growing number of excommunications.

This solution, presented by Hermas as a divine revelation brought by an "angel of Penance" (or "Shepherd", hence the name of the work), offered a second chance of forgiveness to those who had stained themselves, after baptism, with severe

---

[52] Ernesto Buonaiuti, *Storia del Cristianesimo* (Roma: Newton & Compton, 2002), p. 51.

[53] According to Rodney Stark's estimates, from 100 to 140 C.E., Christians increased by an average of 40% every 10 years, reaching about 40,000. Although the percentage, in relation to the estimated population of about 60 million, was only 0.07%, the growth within the communities was about 500% in 40 years. Rodney Stark, *Ascesa e affermazione del cristianesimo* (Torino: Lindau, 2007), 17 ff. In my opinion, these are somewhat too high numerical assessments. Anyway, the growth was certainly enormous and, for the purposes of my hypothesis, it is not strictly necessary to determine the exact percentage of growth.

and public sins.[54]

In the story, in addition to the Angel of Penance, another figure dominates: a venerable lady, a symbol of the Church. The purpose of the book could be summed up with the words that the author puts in the mouth of this character:

μὴ διαλίπῃς οὖν νουθετῶν σου τὰ τέκνα. οἶδα γάρ, ὅτι, ἐὰν μετανοήσουσιν ἐξ ὅλης καρδίας αὐτῶν, ἐνγραφήσονται εἰς τὰς βίβλους τῆς ζωῆς	Cease not therefore to admonish your sons; for I know that, if they repent with all their heart, they will be enrolled in the Books of Life with the saints.[56] (*Shep.* Vis. I:3,2)

---

[54] We could hypothesize that if, as it seems, before Hermas the penitential doctrine was not excessively developed, then this would tend to corroborate the practice of a baptism in old age. As Filoramo confirms: "the difficulty of the trials and the need to no longer fall into a grave sin help, on the other hand, to understand how throughout the period during which the prevailing form of baptism remained that of adults, many preferred to procrastinate this event to the last" - Giovanni Filoramo, Daniele Menozzi, *Storia del Cristianesimo, L'antichità*, (Roma: Editori Laterza, 2001), p. 241. The daily experience of sin of those who "preferred to procrastinate", ended up involving even the baptized, to the point that, at the time of Hermas, the gravity of the moral situation of the entire Christian society, as Buonaiuti paints it, forced our author to present this solution of *paenitentia secunda*. But the keys to interpretation are many; scholars such as Poshmann and Brox "see instead in the Pastor of Hermas nothing more than the codification of an already consolidated ecclesial praxis or even a tightening of the practice of penance restricted to a single and only time" - Hubertus R. Drobner, *Patrologia* (Casale Monferrato: Piemme, 2002), p. 94.

[56] https://www.earlychristianwritings.com/text/shepherd.html. Text amended by me.

| μετὰ τῶν ἁγίων. [55]

This writing by Hermas also offers us interesting food for thought that can help us in our historical analysis. In fact, it is more than evident that the theme of "baptism" is undoubtedly central to revelations. It is said of a quadrangular tower built on the waters:

<table>
<tr><td>

διατί οὖν ἐπὶ
ὑδάτων ᾠκοδόμηται
ὁ πύργος, ἄκουε· ὅτι
ἡ ζωὴ ὑμῶν διὰ
ὕδατος ἐσώθη καὶ
σωθήσεται.[57]

</td><td>

Hear then why the
tower is built upon the
waters. It is because
your life has been, and
will be, saved through
water.[58]
(*Shep.* Vis. III:3,4)

</td></tr>
</table>

The tower depicts the society of the Christian faithful, represented by as many stones of different shapes and conditions, depending on the moral and religious qualities of each one. All of them, however, contribute equally to constitute the symbolic building from which those who have fallen into guilt are excluded.

The "waters" on which the tower is built are a symbol for baptism, which, throughout the work, is also designated by the writer with a word widely used by Christianity of the second century, namely "the seal":

<table>
<tr><td>

ἡ σφραγὶς οὖν τὸ
ὕδωρ ἐστίν· εἰς τὸ
ὕδωρ οὖν

</td><td>

The seal, then, is the
water: they descend
into the water dead,

</td></tr>
</table>

---

[55] https://www.ccel.org/l/lake/fathers/shepherd_a.htm.
[57] https://www.ccel.org/l/lake/fathers/shepherd_b.htm.
[58] See footnote 55.

<table>
<tr><td>

καταβαινουσι νεκροὶ καὶ ἀναβαίνουσι ζῶντες. κἀκείνοις οὖν ἐκηρύχθη ἡ σφραγὶς αὕτη καὶ ἐχρήσαντο αὐτῇ, ἵνα εἰσέλθωσιν εἰς τὴν βασιλείαν τοῦ θεοῦ.[59]

</td><td>

and they arise alive. And to them, accordingly, was this seal preached, and they made use of it that they might enter into the kingdom of God.[60]
(*Shep*. Sim. 9: XVI:4)

</td></tr>
</table>

As from the writings examined above, it is also possible to derive only clues from this, however useful. There is no explicit mention of the baptism of infants, but everything seems to be moving in the opposite direction. For example, we read of the consequence of listening to the word and the subsequent desire to be "baptized":

<table>
<tr><td>

οὗτοί εἰσιν οἱ τὸν λόγον ἀκούσαντες καὶ θέλοντες βαπτισθῆναι εἰς τὸ ὄνομα τοῦ κυρίου[61]

</td><td>

These are they who have heard the word and wish to be baptized in the name of the Lord.[62]
(*Shep*. Vis. III:7,3)

</td></tr>
</table>

That is, it is a choice of conversion made in full awareness, a choice to which no newborn can, of course, be subjected.

Speaking of the one who, after receiving the "seal" of baptism, sins but sincerely repents, Hermas writes:

---

[59] https://www.ccel.org/l/lake/fathers/shepherd_g.htm.
[60] See footnote 56.
[61] https://www.ccel.org/l/lake/fathers/shepherd_b.htm.
[62] See footnote 56.

"for although any of them be tempted by the most wicked devil and commit sin, he will quickly return to his Lord.
I deem you happy, I, who am the messenger of repentance, whoever of you are innocent as children because your part is good and honourable before God".[63]
(*Shep.* Sim. IX:31,2-3)

Here too, as in the case of the *Letter of Barnabas*, we note the significant parallelism between a post-baptismal condition approved by Christ and the condition of "innocence" of children. We could ask ourselves if the state of children was not also understood as a post-baptismal condition, but a careful examination of the Pastor does not allow us to move in this direction. Hermas says:

ἔδει γὰρ τὸν εἰληφότα ἄφεσιν ἁμαρτιῶν μηκέτι ἁμαρτάνειν, ἀλλ' ἐν ἁγνείᾳ κατοικεῖν [64]	For he who has received the remission of his sins ought not to sin any more, but to live in purity.[65] (*Shep.* Prec. IV:3,2)

Those who have been baptized and have received the forgiveness of sins must strive to remain in a state of purity. In addition:

Ἁπλότητα ἔχε καὶ ἄκακος γίνου, καὶ ἔσῃ ὡς τὰ νήπια τὰ μὴ γινώσκοντα τὴν	Be simple and guileless, and you will be as the children who know not the wickedness that ruins the life

---

[63] *Ibidem.* This lost portion of the Greek text has come down to us through Latin translations only.
[64] https://www.ccel.org/l/lake/fathers/shepherd_c.htm.
[65] See footnote 56.

| πονηρίαν τὴν
ἀπολλύουσαν τὴν ζωὴν
τῶν ἀνθρώπων[66] | of men.[67]
(*Shep.* Prec. II:1) |

Anyone who manages to remain in this state of post-baptismal purity will find himself in the same condition as children who "do not know the wickedness that destroys life". But if these children had been in a post-baptismal state, Hermas' whole speech would have made little sense.

Many other scholars, including Kurt Aland[68], have come to the same conclusion. In their opinion, the sub-apostolic authors would have drawn their conviction about the concept of "purity" of children directly from the words of the apostle Paul:

| ἡγίασται γὰρ ὁ ἀνὴρ ὁ ἄπιστος ἐν τῇ γυναικὶ καὶ ἡγίασται ἡ γυνὴ ἡ ἄπιστος ἐν τῷ ἀδελφῷ· ἐπεὶ ἄρα τὰ τέκνα ὑμῶν ἀκάθαρτά ἐστιν, νῦν δὲ ἅγιά ἐστιν.[69] | For the unbelieving husband is made holy through his wife, and the unbelieving wife is made holy through the brother. Otherwise, your children would be unclean, but as it is, they are holy.[70] |

Indeed, it is necessary to point out that, if it had been typical to baptize children, they would hardly have needed the merit of the believing parent to be extended to them.

We have thus concluded the examination of these first three works: the *Didache*, the *Letter of Barnabas* and the *Shepherd of*

---

[66] https://www.ccel.org/l/lake/fathers/shepherd_c.htm.

[67] https://www.earlychristianwritings.com/text/shepherd.html.

[68] Kurt Aland, *Op. Cit.*, p. 29 ff.

[69] NA28.

[70] 1 Corinthians 7:14 (NRSVUE).

Hermas. What we can certainly say is that not only is there no explicit reference to forms of paedobaptism but, above all, that every clue or hint of baptism seems to apply only to adult persons. The same conclusion can be drawn from the examination of all other contemporary Christian documents.

Anyone who disagrees with the above statements can only support the practice of infant baptism in the early second century as *argumentum ex silentio*.

Chapter II

Apology of Aristides of Athens

Although dated to the same period in which the letter of Barnabas was written, Aristides' work needs to be classified together with apologetic writings.[71] These featured in Christian communities from the middle of the second century so that, once strengthened, they were able to direct their attention towards external society, carrying out

> "equally decisive and systematic attempts to present the salient elements of the Christian message to the public, whose basic vision of the world was based on the tradition of Greek philosophical thought accumulated up to that moment".[72]

Critics in general label Aristides' apology as not particularly original nor a work of great depth,

> "[but] the interest of the writing is precisely in this first use of the philosophical critique of religion by a Christian author".[73]

Who was this proto-apologist Christian? What features does his writing present? And above all, what did he say that was

---

[71] According to theologian Alister McGrath, apologetics can be defined as that "Area of Christian theology that focuses on the defence of the Christian faith, especially through the rational justification of Christian belief and doctrine.", cf. Alister McGrath, *Op. Cit.*, p. 565.

[72] David T. Runia, Roberto Radice, *Op. Cit.*, p. 105.

[73] Giorgio Jossa, *Il cristianesimo antico. Dalle origini al concilio di Nicea* (Roma: Carocci editore, 2007), p. 92.

relevant for the baptism of infants?

Aristides was a philosopher from Athens, as he himself defines himself in the title of the work; the very little information we have about him comes to us mainly through Eusebius, who writes:

> "Aristides also, a believer earnestly devoted to our religion, left, like Quadratus, an apology for the faith, addressed to Adrian. His work, too, has been preserved even to the present day by a great many persons".[74]

Carlotta Alpigiano, in her critical edition, affirms that it is

> "[...] very likely that Aristides at least attended some philosophical school, both because the approach of his discourse is [...] philosophical, and because he insists on an experience of research prior to conversion that could indicate his approach to some philosophy".[75]

The above is to be contrasted with the opinion of other scholars who consider it probable that Aristides used the term "philosopher" in a broad sense, as was the custom in the second century. Certainly, Aristides was a pagan convert who may have previously adhered to Judaism[76] but who ultimately came, through reflection, to embrace the Christian faith.

His work has come to us through the following sources:

---

[74] https://www.newadvent.org/fathers/250104.htm. Cf. Franzo Migliore, *Historia Ecclesiastica* IV.3.3, *Eusebio di Cesarea, storia ecclesiastica/1* (Roma: Città Nuova Editrice, 2005), p. 195.

[75] Carlotta Alpigiano, *Aristides di Atene. Apologia* (Firenze: Nardini editore, 1988), p. 8 ftn 4.

[76] This is the general opinion of critics, motivated by the unusual favorable disposition that the author shows towards the Jews. Cf *ibid.*, p. 13.

- papyrus fragment *P. Oxy. 1778, (fourth century)*
- papyrus fragment *P. Lit. Lond. 223, (fourth century)*
- novel *Barlaam et Joasaph*, generally attributed to John Damascene (ca. 650-749 C.E.), which came to us thanks to multiple witnesses. Here the apology appears in chap. 37, anonymously and in an adapted version, in the form of a speech delivered by the soothsayer Nachor
- *Syriac version (fourth century), from Cod. Syr. 16, (seventh century)*
- *Armenian version* (first two chapters) from a Venetian manuscript *(tenth century)*
- *Armenian version,* from a manuscript of Edschmiazin *(eleventh century)*

For an examination of the main differences between these sources, I refer to the critical edition of Alpigiano[77]; for our purposes, I limit myself to indicating the divergence between the Armenian version, which, together with Eusebius, indicates the emperor Hadrian (117–138 C.E.) as the recipient, and the Syriac version which contains a real dedication addressed to "Titus Hadrian Antoninus", that is, the emperor Antoninus Pius (138-161 C.E.).

As you can well understand, being able to establish the correct recipient is essential to date the work. The criticism is not unanimous and the discussions on this are vast.

If Alpigiano is correct, then:

> "the Apology would have been written at the time of Hadrian, but the death of the sovereign having occurred in the meantime, would have resulted in the author reviewing the dedication and presenting it to his

---

[77] I also recommend comparing Bernard Pouderon, *Apologie* (Paris: Cerf, 2003).

successor. Copies dating back to one and to the other edition of the dedication would then be disseminated".[78]

The general scheme of the Apology can be represented in six lines of argumentation:

a)   the existence of God – chap.1
b)   mankind is divided into lineages – chap. 2
c)   the falsity of religion and the god of the barbarians is demonstrated – chap. 3-7
d)   the falsity of religion and the Greek gods is demonstrated – chap. 8-13
e)   Judaism is criticized – chap.14
f)   Christianity is the people who have found the truth about God – chap.15-17

There is only one point in all the work that is useful to our end, but I believe that its importance is highly relevant. This is Ar. 15:4 which, according to the Alpigiano edition, reports[79]:

---

[78] Carlotta Alpigiano, *Op. Cit.*, p. 130.
[79] *Ibid.*, pp. 116-117.

From Greek[80] (*P. Lit. Lond. 223, fourth century*)	**From Syriac** (*Cod. Syr. 16, fourth century*)
their women are pure and virgins and they haven't offered their wombs; their men abstain from all illegitimate sexual intercourse and impurity, and still more their women abstain likewise: for they cling to the great hope to come. But also their slaves or their young servants, if they have any, or their children, they persuade them to become Christians to make them benevolent, and, when they have become such, they call them brothers, with no divisions.	and their wives, O king, are pure as virgins, and their daughters are modest: and their men abstain from all unlawful wedlock and from all impurity, in the hope of the recompense that is to come in another world: but as for their servants or handmaids, or their children, if any of them have any, they persuade them to become Christians for the love that they have towards them; and when they have become so, they call them without distinction brethren[81]

[80] καὶ αἱ γυναῖκες αὐτῶν ἁγναὶ καὶ παρθένοι εἰσιν, καὶ ταῖς γαστράσιν οὐκ ὑποτιθέασιν, οἱ δὲ ἄνδρες αὐτῶν ἐγκρατεύονται ἀπὸ πάσης συνουσίας ἀνόμου καὶ ἀκαθαρσίας, μᾶλλον δὲ καὶ αἱ γυναῖκες ὁμοίως ἐγκρατεύονται, ἐλπίδος γὰρ μεγάλης ἀντέχονται τῆς μελλούσης, ἀλλὰ καὶ δούλους ἢ παιδίσκας ἐὰν ἔχωσιν ἢ τέκνα, πείθουσιν αὐτοὺς χριστιανοὺς γενέσθαι, ἵνα ἔχωσιν εὔνους, καὶ ὅταν γένωνται τοιοῦτοι ἀδελφοὺς καλοῦσιν αὐτοὺς ἀμέριστοι ὄντες.

[81] James Rendel Harris, Joseph Armitage Robinson, *The apology of Aristides on behalf of the Christians* (Cambridge: University Press, 1893), p. 49.

In this passage, Aristides praises some characteristics of Christians that have a positive social impact. He affirms that if these Christians have servants or children, they persuade them, instruct them, so that they too may become Christians and only then be called "brothers without distinction". This use of calling oneself αδελφοι was notoriously mocked by pagans[82], but among Christians, it was indicative of a close spiritual relationship. This would seem to be an extraordinary piece of evidence that excludes infant baptism because it clearly states that children must first be persuaded and instructed and only then "become Christians".

Aland draws the same conclusion:

> "The impression given is that [children] are baptized only
> after obtaining the necessary understanding, so not before
> they have reached a certain age".[83]

A question that must be asked is: are we sure that Aristides was not talking about the children of servants rather than the children of Christians? One might think that the text contains an ambiguity. If we analyze another critical edition, the one edited by Harris, who discovered the Syriac version, and by Robinson, who identified the text in the novel by Barlaam et Joasaph, we note that the passage is rendered in the following way by the Syriac version:

> "but as for their servants or handmaids, or their children,
> if any of them have any, they persuade them to become

---

[82] Tertullian, in his *Apology* (39:8), speaking of the attitude of the pagans states: "as for the fact that we are called brothers, I believe that what makes them unreasonable is because with them every title of kinship is synonymous with unfelt affection".

[83] Kurt Aland, *Op. Cit.*, p. 57.

Christians [...]".[84]

In relation to the Greek version, Kurt Aland states that the text

"makes it impossible to understand the τέκνα as children
of the servants. According to Aristides, then, a baptism of
these children while still infants is excluded".[85]

While the writings examined above (Didache, letter of Barnabas, Pastor of Hermas) were addressed to the Christian society itself, and therefore it was unnecessary to clearly explain the path that led to baptism, with the Apologies, particularly that of Aristides, it was necessary to provide more details because the recipients of such writings were, or were supposed to be, in a position of total ignorance. If Aristides provides us with the interesting information mentioned above, we would also expect to find further, equally clear information from the later apologetic writings of Justin Martyr.

---

[84] James Rendel Harris, Joseph Armitage Robinson, *The apology of Aristides on behalf of the Christians* (Cambridge: University Press, 1893), p. 49.
[85] Kurt Aland, *Op. Cit.*, p. 57.

Justin is, if not the most important, definitely the best-known apologist of the second century. He was born around 100 C.E.[86] in Flavia Neapolis, near ancient Shechem, near present-day Nablus. Descended from settlers who came to Palestine after the destruction of Jerusalem in 70 C.E., he was educated in Greek philosophy but converted to Christianity at the age of 33, thanks to the testimony of an elderly Christian

> "which some scholars identify as Polycarp of Smyrna, who had been a direct disciple of the Apostle John".[87]

Not everyone agrees with this identification, but if it were the case, then the teachings of Justin would be directly traceable to those of the apostles through a single intermediary. Be that as it may, thanks to his Palestinian origins, he was able to confront both Jewish and Greek cultures. But as Giuseppe Visonà points out,

> "it seems, however, that Justin was not greatly influenced by the environment of origin, as evidenced by the fact that he did not know Hebrew, as repeatedly appears from the discussions about OT reported in the *Dialogue*".[88]

Fifteen years after his conversion, in 148 C.E., Justin moved to Rome, where he opened a school to teach his philosophy.

---

[86] Giuseppe Girgenti, *Giustino – Apologie* (Milano: Rusconi Libri, 1995), p. 31.

[87] *Ibid.*, p. 14.

[88] Giuseppe Visonà, *Dialogo con Trifone* (Milano: Edizioni Paoline, 1988), p. 15 ftn. 1.

Covered by the *pallium*, which he is said to have worn on every occasion, he devoted himself to the teaching and defence of the Christian faith until his death sentence, which took place in the year 165 C.E. by order of the prefect Junius Rusticus, who ruled during the empire of Marcus Aurelius, from 163 to 167 C.E. The execution probably took place following a denunciation of the cynical philosopher Crescens[89].

Justin's literary production was very vast. The only three complete works recognized as authentic that have come down to us are:

- First Apology
- Second Apology
- Dialogue with Tryphon

Unfortunately, these are entrusted to a single codex, the *Parisinus Graecus 450*, dated to 1364 C.E. This code contains numerous other works attributed to Justin but is considered inauthentic by modern textual criticism. As Giuseppe Girgenti points out,

> "[the] apologies and dialogue with Tryphon are certainly authentic. All the others are considered spurious for reasons of internal criticism of the text (style and thought); however, there is no reason for external criticism, indeed, on the contrary, three other titles coincide with those named by Eusebius, and there is also a certain correspondence between the content of the same and the description handed down by Eusebius".[90]

In reality, there is only one actual Apology, that is, the first, dated around 150 C.E. and addressed to Antoninus Pius and his

---

[89] Giuseppe Girgenti, *Op. Cit.*, p. 14.
[90] *Ibid.*, p.16.

sons Lucius Verus (adopted son) and Marcus Aurelius (associated with the empire in 138 C.E., with the title of Caesar). Giuseppe Visonà confirms that

> "the so-called II Apology, much shorter (15 chapters against 68) and without address, is commonly considered an appendix of the first (as such the Goodspeed publishes it) or an autonomous but more episodic and occasional writing".[91]

According to the structure reported by Girgenti[92], the First Apology could be schematized as follows:

a) Introduction
b) Analysis of accusations against Christians
c) Defence and description of the faith
d) Comparison between Hellenism and Christianity
e) Condemnation of idolatry and heresies
f) Condemnation of immorality
g) Messianic prophecies about Christ
h) The Doctrine of the Logos
i) Other prophecies about the future
j) Jews and Gentiles
k) Heretics
l) Platonism and Christianity
m) Baptism
n) Revelation and pagan mythology
o) The Holy Mass and the Eucharist
p) The rescript of Adriano and Minucio Fundano

In chapters 61 and 62 especially, Justin addresses the

---

[91] Giuseppe Visonà, *Op. Cit.*, p. 18.
[92] Giuseppe Girgenti, *Op. Cit.*, p. 27.

discourse on baptism. He writes:

Ὃν τρόπον δὲ καὶ ἀνεθήκαμεν ἑαυτοὺς τῷ θεῷ καινοποιηθέντες διὰ τοῦ Χριστοῦ, ἐξηγησόμεθα, ὅπως μὴ τοῦτο παραλιπόντες δόξωμεν πονηρεύειν τι ἐν τῇ ἐξηγήσει. (*Apol.* 1, LXI:1)	I will also relate the manner in which we dedicated ourselves to God when we were made new through Christ; lest, if we omit this, we seem to be unfair in the explanation we are making.[93]

To avoid talking about baptism would be for Justin a serious gap in his exposition. Thus he goes on to explain the "way" in which a Christian consecrates himself to God. We would expect him to include infant baptism if this were one of the "ways" of consecrating oneself to the Lord. But he makes no mention of it. Indeed he goes on to state:

ὅσοι ἂν πεισθῶσι καὶ πιστεύωσιν ἀληθῆ ταῦτα τὰ ὑφ' ἡμῶν διδασκόμενα καὶ λεγόμενα εἶναι, καὶ βιοῦν οὕτως δύνασθαι ὑπισχνῶνται,	As many as are persuaded and believe that what we teach and say is true, and undertake to be able to live accordingly, they are instructed to pray and to entreat God with fasting for the remission of their

---

[93] https://earlywritings.com/forum/viewtopic.php?f=3&t=1874#p41230. Translation amended by me.

> εὔχεσθαί τε καὶ αἰτεῖν νηστεύοντες παρὰ τοῦ θεοῦ τῶν προημαρτημένων ἄφεσιν διδάσκονται, ἡμῶν συνευχομένων καὶ συννηστευόντων αὐτοῖς.
>
> (*Apol.* 1, LXI:2)

> past sins, while we pray and fast with them.[94]

The need for a preliminary "education" in the faith is highlighted, for a catechetical path that only "later" leads to baptism:

> ἔπειτα ἄγονται ὑφ' ἡμῶν ἔνθα ὕδωρ ἐστί, καὶ τρόπον ἀναγεννήσεως, ὃν καὶ ἡμεῖς αὐτοὶ ἀνεγεννήθημεν, ἀναγεννῶνται· ἐπ' ὀνόματος γὰρ τοῦ πατρὸς τῶν ὅλων καὶ δεσπότου θεοῦ καὶ τοῦ σωτῆρος ἡμῶν Ἰησοῦ Χριστοῦ καὶ πνεύματος ἁγίου τὸ ἐν

> Then they are brought by us where there is water, and they are regenerated in the same manner in which we were ourselves regenerated. For, in the name of God, the Father and Lord of the universe, and of our Saviour Jesus Christ, and of the Holy Spirit, they then receive the washing with water.[95]

---

[94] *Ibidem.*
[95] *Ibidem.*

τῷ ὕδατι τότε λουτρὸν
ποιοῦνται.
(*Apol.* I, LXI:3)

Is it possible that Justin neglects to speak of the baptism of infants for another reason? Or is it possible that, while not speaking about it in this specific section of his apology, he mentions this practice in his other works?

According to some scholars, there seem to be clear "baptismal resonances"[96] in many points of the *Dialogue with Tryphon*, where Justin repeatedly compares the practice of Jewish circumcision, which took place on the eighth day after the birth of each child, to the baptismal practice of the Christian. For example, speaking of the first, he states:

ὁρᾶτε ὡς οὐ ταύτην τὴν περιτομὴν τὴν εἰς σημεῖον δοθεῖσαν ὁ θεὸς θέλει· οὐδὲ γὰρ Αἰγυπτίοις χρήσιμος οὐδὲ τοῖς υἱοῖς Μωάβ οὐδὲ τοῖς υἱοῖς Ἐδώμ. ἀλλὰ κἂν Σκύθης ᾖ τις ἢ Πέρσης, ἔχει δὲ τὴν τοῦ θεοῦ γνῶσιν καὶ τοῦ Χριστοῦ αὐτοῦ καὶ φυλάσσει τὰ αἰώνια δίκαια, περιτέτμηται τὴν καλὴν καὶ

Do you see how that God does not mean this circumcision which is given for a sign? For it is of no use to the Egyptians, or the sons of Moab, or the sons of Edom. But even if a man is Scythian or Persian, if he has the knowledge of God and of His Christ, and keeps the everlasting righteous decrees, he is circumcised with the good and useful circumcision and is a friend of God, and God

---

[96] Giuseppe Visonà, *Op. Cit.*, p. 115 ftn. 4.

<table>
<tr><td>

ὠφέλιμον περιτομήν,
καὶ φίλος ἐστὶ τῷ θεῷ,
καὶ ἐπὶ τοῖς δώροις
αὐτοῦ καὶ ταῖς
προσφοραῖς χαίρει.[97]

</td><td>

rejoices in his gifts and
offerings.[98]

</td></tr>
</table>

The mention that Justin makes, a few sentences before, relating to "conversion":

<table>
<tr><td>

μὴ ὑπερτίθεσθε μηδὲ
διστάζετε πιστεῦσαι τῷ
ἀπεριτμήτῳ ἐμοί. βραχὺς
οὗτος ὑμῖν περιλείπεται
προσηλύσεως χρόνος.
(*Dial.* XXVIII:2)

</td><td>

do not delay or hesitate to
put faith in me, although I
am an uncircumcised man;
so short a time is left you in
which to become
proselytes.[99]

</td></tr>
</table>

and the fact that he speaks of literal circumcision as a "sign" to be opposed to "just circumcision" would seem to confirm Justin's willingness to compare the practice of circumcision with that of Christian baptism. But a correct exegesis of these passages does not historically support paedobaptism with the writings of Justin. Rather than a parallel between Jewish and Christian praxis, he seems to repeatedly highlight its antithesis.

<table>
<tr><td>

μακάριοι οὖν ἡμεῖς οἱ
περιτμηθέντες πετρίναις
μαχαίραις τὴν δευτέραν

</td><td>

Blessed, therefore, are we
who have been circumcised
the second time with knives
of stone. For your first

</td></tr>
</table>

---

[97] *Dialogue With Trypho* XXVIII:4.
[98] See footnote 93.
[99] *Ibidem.*

περιτομήν. ὑμῶν μὲν γὰρ ἡ πρώτη διὰ σιδήρου γέγονε καὶ γίνεται· σκληροκάρδιοι γὰρ μένετε· ἡμῶν δὲ ἡ περιτομή, ἥτις δευτέρα ἀριθμῷ, μετὰ τὴν ὑμετέραν φανερωθεῖσα, διὰ λίθων ἀκροτόμων, τοῦτ' ἔστι διὰ τῶν λόγων τῶν διὰ τῶν ἀποστόλων τοῦ ἀκρογωνιαίου λίθου καὶ τοῦ ἄνευ χειρῶν τμηθέντος.
(*Dial.* CXIV:4)

circumcision was and is performed by iron instruments, for you remain hard-hearted; but our circumcision, which is the second, having been instituted after yours, circumcises us from idolatry and from absolutely every kind of wickedness by sharp stones, i.e., by the words [preached] by the apostles of the corner-stone cut out without hands.[100]

In this last quotation, Justin again contrasts the "second circumcision" with the first, that is, with the literal circumcision of the Jews.

For Christians, the instrument to produce this "circumcision" is not a literal iron knife but is produced through a "stone knife", which symbolizes the apostolic announcement.[101] The "second circumcision" of a Christian, namely his baptism, is the fruit of the "words proclaimed through the apostles"; that is, it follows a catechetical work. That Justin has baptism in mind seems to be corroborated by the following sentences:

---

[100] *Ibidem.*

[101] A probable reference to the apostles as "stones" upon which the Church of God is built.

ἀλλὰ ταῦτα μὲν οὐ νοεῖτε λέγοντος· ἃ γὰρ ποιῆσαι τὸν Χριστὸν πεπροφήτευται οὐ νενοήκατε, οὐδὲ ἡμῖν προσάγουσιν ὑμᾶς τοῖς γεγραμμένοις πιστεύετε. Ἰερεμίας μὲν γὰρ οὕτω βοᾷ· Οὐαὶ ὑμῖν, ὅτι ἐγκατελίπετε πηγὴν ζῶσαν καὶ ὠρύξατε ἑαυτοῖς λάκκους συντετριμμένους, οἳ οὐ δυνήσονται συνέχειν ὕδωρ. Μὴ ἔρημον ᾖ οὗ ἐστι τὸ ὄρος Σιών; ὅτι Ἰερουσαλὴμ βιβλίον ἀποστασίου ἔδωκα ἔμπροσθεν ὑμῶν.
(*Dial.* CXIV:5)

But you do not comprehend me when I speak these things; for you have not understood what it has been prophesied that Christ would do, and you do not believe us who draw your attention to what has been written. For Jeremiah thus cries: 'Woe unto you! because you have forsaken the living fountain, and have dug for yourselves broken cisterns that can hold no water. Shall there be a wilderness where Mount Zion is, because I gave Jerusalem a bill of divorce in your sight?[102]

Visonà comments on this last sentence as follows:

"A quotation composed of Jer 2:12-13 and Is 16:1-2 is found, in baptismal context, in Ps. Barnabas, *Epistle* 11:2-3 [..]. That of Justin is therefore certainly a composite *testimonium* formed in the context of the anti-ritualistic polemic, and that for the baptismal resonances of Jer 2:13 was also used in relation to baptism (cf. *Dial.*

---

[102] See footnote 93.

14,1; 19,2; 140,1)".[103]

To increase the contrast between literal circumcision and Christian baptism, Justin reports:

καὶ τὸ μὴ δύνασθαι δὲ τὸ θῆλυ γένος τὴν σαρκικὴν περιτομὴν λαμβάνειν δείκνυσιν ὅτι εἰς σημεῖον ἡ περιτομὴ αὕτη δέδοται, ἀλλ' οὐχ ὡς ἔργον δικαιοσύνης (*Dial.* XXIII:5)	Furthermore, the inability of the female sex to receive fleshly circumcision, proves that this circumcision has been given for a sign, and not for a work of righteousness.[104]

It is baptism that works the "justification". And again:

Ἰησοῦς Χριστὸς πάντας τοὺς βουλομένους περιτέμνει, ὥσπερ ἄνωθεν ἐκηρύσσετο, πετρίναις μαχαίραις, ἵνα γένηται ἔθνος δίκαιον, λαὸς φυλάσσων πίστιν, ἀντιλαμβανόμενος	Jesus Christ circumcises all who will--as was declared above--with knives of stone; that they may be a righteous nation, a people keeping the faith, holding to the truth, and maintaining peace.[105]

---

[103] Giuseppe Visonà, *Op. Cit.*, p. 330, ftn. 2.
[104] See footnote 93.
[105] *Ibidem.*

> ἀληθείας καὶ φυλάσσων
> εἰϱήνην.
> (*Dial.* XXIV:22)

Returning to his first Apology, Justin introduces in verse IV the concept of the new birth: "If you are not born again, you will not enter the kingdom of heaven". [106]
The reference to the Gospel of John seems quite clear:

> "Jesus answered, 'Very truly, I tell you, no one can enter the kingdom of God without being born of water and Spirit'".[107]

Justin goes on to the next verse, saying:

> ὅτι δὲ καὶ ἀδύνατον
> εἰς τὰς μήτϱας τῶν
> τεκουσῶν τοὺς
> ἅπαξ γενομένους
> ἐμβῆναι, φανεϱὸν
> πᾶσίν ἐστι.
> (*Apol.* 1, LXI:5)

Now, that it is impossible for those who have once been born to enter into their mothers' wombs is manifest to all. [108]

Thanks to this last quote, we can say that we are sure that he was referring to the episode of Nicodemus:

> "Nicodemus said to him, 'How can anyone be born after having grown old? Can one enter a second time into the mother's womb and be born?'".[109]

---

[106] Giuseppe Girgenti, *Apol.* 1, LXI:5, in *Op. cit.*, p. 157.
[107] John 3:5 (NRSVUE)
[108] See footnote 93.
[109] John 3:4 (NRSVUE)

According to Giuseppe Girgenti, it is also possible to suppose a connection[110] with the Gospel of Matthew:

> "and said, 'Truly I tell you, unless you change and become like children, you will never enter the kingdom of heaven'"[111].

From the above, one might think that a child's status is pointed out as an ideal, or at least acceptable, condition for approaching the sacrament of baptism.

Bruno Corsani sheds light on the meaning of these Gospel verses by explaining that:

> "the child indicates the stage of development of the human person who does not yet claim his own merits but depends on the gift, love and care of others".[112]

Then he goes on to state:

> "Becoming like little children does not mean, therefore, retracing an impossible road backwards, returning to one's past, but it means stripping oneself of all merit and pretension, receiving the Kingdom in listening to the gospel of grace offered to sinners and the unworthy (Cf. John 3,3.7)".[113]

The "child", therefore, is seen as "an image of the condition for entering the Kingdom".[114] It does not seem convincing to

---

[110] Giuseppe Girgenti, *Op. cit.*, 255, note 225.
[111] Matthew 18:3 (NRSVUE)
[112] Bruno Corsani, *I vangeli sinottici* (Torino: Claudiana, 2008), p. 171.
[113] *Ibid.*, pp. 171-172.
[114] *Ibidem.*

deduce, from the juxtaposition between these verses and the words of Justin, any conclusion on paedobaptesimal praxis; "to be born again", was simply a symbol and expression of Christian *metanoia*. It is he himself who removes all doubts about it when he writes:

Original Greek[115]	*English translation*[116]
καὶ λόγον δὲ εἰς τοῦτο παρὰ τῶν ἀποστόλων ἐμάθομεν τοῦτον. ἐπειδὴ τὴν πρώτην γένεσιν ἡμῶν ἀγνοοῦντες κατ' ἀνάγκην γεγεννήμεθα ἐξ ὑγρᾶς σπορᾶς κατὰ μῖξιν τὴν τῶν γονέων πρὸς ἀλλήλους καὶ ἐν ἔθεσι φαύλοις καὶ πονηραῖς ἀνατροφαῖς γεγόναμεν, ὅπως μὴ ἀνάγκης τέκνα μηδὲ ἀγνοίας μένωμεν ἀλλὰ προαιρέσεως καὶ ἐπιστήμης, ἀφέσεώς τε ἁμαρτιῶν ὑπὲρ ὧν προημάρτομεν τύχωμεν, ἐν τῷ ὕδατι	And for this rite, we have learned from the apostles this reason. Since at our birth we were born without our own knowledge or choice, by our parents coming together, and were brought up in bad habits and wicked training; in order that we may not remain the children of necessity and of ignorance, but may become the children of choice and knowledge, and may obtain in the water the remission of sins formerly committed, there is pronounced over him who chooses to be born again, and has repented of his sins, the name of God the Father and Lord of the universe; he who leads to the layer the person that is to be washed calling him by this name alone.

---

[115] *Apol.* 1, LXI:9, 10.
[116] See footnote 93.

> ἐπονομάζεται τῷ
> ἑλομένῳ ἀναγεννηθῆναι
> καὶ μετανοήσαντι ἐπὶ
> τοῖς ἡμαρτημένοις τὸ τοῦ
> πατρὸς τῶν ὅλων καὶ
> δεσπότου θεοῦ ὄνομα,
> αὐτὸ τοῦτο μόνον
> ἐπιλέγοντος τοῦ τὸν
> λουσόμενον ἄγοντος ἐπὶ
> τὸ λουτρόν.

Justin clearly states that baptism must take place exactly the opposite of how the actual birth of an individual takes place. Since we were born "ignorant out of necessity" because our birth was not wanted by us but by our parents, then in order not to remain "children of ignorance" but to become "children of wisdom" and obtain "the remission of sins", we must consciously "decide to be born again" by submitting to baptism.

Such a contrast between the birth of a child that takes place by the decision of others, that is, of the "parents", and the birth of a Christian which takes place in awareness and "wisdom", leaves very little room for any hypothesis that historically supports the practice of paedobaptism in Justin through parallelism with the circumcision of Jewish infants. In fact, Kurt Aland declares that:

> "[Justin's first apology] probably presupposes adults [baptism] exclusively, but certainly not infants".[117]

---

[117] Kurt Aland, *Op. Cit.*, p. 54.

With the subsequent balanced affirmation of Professor Fulvio Ferrario, professor of Systematic Theology at the Waldensian Faculty of Theology, we conclude the examination of those historical documents that characterized the central period of the second century and we enter the period from the end of the II to the beginning of the III:

> "The baptism of children (paedobaptism) is not widely practised before 160 C.E.: the statements [...] *contrary do not seem to reflect the documentary evidence.* The oldest written testimonies of the baptism of children date back to the third century".[118]

---

[118] Fulvio Ferrario, *Libertà di credere* (Torino: Claudiana, 2000), p. 218 (italics added).

Chapter III

Against Heresies by Irenaeus of Lyons

Like Justin, Irenaeus, although not generally counted among apologists, plays a decisive role in the history of ancient Christianity. He is often referred to as "the most important of the theologians of the second century".[119]

He is supposed to have been born around 130 C.E.[120], although some critics set the date of birth between 140 C.E. and 160 C.E.[121], and died shortly after 200 C.E., at the age of about 70.[122] Important information is obtained through Eusebius, who reports an excerpt from the letter sent by Irenaeus to Florinus, priest[123] of the church of Rome, which reads:

> "I saw you, in fact, when I was still a boy, in Lower Asia following Polycarp [...] they are also able to relate the places where Blessed Polycarp sat down to talk, [I remember] his way of starting and ending a topic; [I remember] the type of life he led, his physical appearance, [I remember] the speeches he held in front of the crowd, the way he told of his relationships with John

---

[119] Johannes Quasten, *Patrologia. I primi due secoli (II-III)* (Casale: Marietti editore, 1980), p. 255.

[120] Giorgio Maschio, *Contro le eresie e gli altri scritti* (Milano: Jaca Book, 1997), 27.

[121] Johannes Quasten, *Op. Cit.*, p. 255.

[122] Cfr Vittorino Dellagiacoma, *Contro le eresie, volume primo* (Siena: Edizioni Cantagalli, 1996), p. 11.

[123] From the Greek πρεσβύτερος (presbyteros) and from the Latin presbyter, literally "elder", most often transliterated to "priest".

and others who had seen the Lord [...]".[124]

Since Polycarp was bishop in the city of Smyrna, where he died a martyr under Marcus Aurelius around 166 CE[125], we can reasonably deduce that Smyrna was the birthplace of Irenaeus. Eusebius also informs us that, just like Justin, Irenaeus also had contact with the apostolic age through Polycarp, a disciple of the apostle John[126]. For unknown reasons, he left Asia Minor and moved to Gaul, where he became a priest in Lyon. The main work, and certainly the best known, of Irenaeus is usually designated with the title of *Adversus haereses* (Against heresies)[127] and consists of two parts. In the first, known as Book I,

> "Irenaeus begins with a detailed analysis of the doctrine of the Valentinians, interspersing it with polemical notes. Only after that does he face the beginnings of Gnosticism".[128]

---

[124] Franzo Migliore, *Historia Ecclesiastica* V.20.5-6 in *Op. Cit.*, p. 295.

[125] Cf Giorgio Jossa, *Op. Cit.*, p. 131.

[126] These "contacts" with the apostolic age must not lead us to think that Irenaeus, Justin, or anyone else who has boasted such references, is free from errors, even gross, in the exposition of their theses. Sometimes these are narrative inaccuracies, other times we are faced with real inexplicable narratives. A typical example to be attributed to Irenaeus is the attempt that he makes, through an articulated exegetical exposition, to prove that Jesus Christ died at the age of 50 (cf. *Against Heresies*, II, 22, 5-6). Irenaeus, to counter the value that the Gnostic teaching on the Aeons attributed to the number 30, voluntarily distances himself from the Gospel narratives attributable to the age in which Jesus died. It is therefore good to clarify that boasting "disciples of a disciple of an apostle" is not enough to evade historical criticism. And this applies, of course, also to the question of paedobaptism (cf Giorgio Maschio, *Op. Cit.*, p. 591, ftn. 3).

[127] The title indeed reported in the writing is "On the Detection and Overthrow of the So-Called Gnosis".

[128] Johannes Quasten, *Op. cit.,* p. 257.

The second is, in turn, divided into four books:

> "Book II refutes Valentinian and Marcionite gnosis with
> arguments of reason;
> Book III, with the Church's doctrine on God and Christ;
> Book IV, with the words of the Lord;
> Book V deals almost exclusively with the resurrection of
> the flesh, denied by all the Gnostics".[129]

In what period can we place the drafting? Irenaeus himself
gives us a useful clue:

> "After Anicetus was succeeded by Soter, now, in twelfth
> place starting with the apostles, he holds the function of
> the episcopate Eleutero [*sic*]".[130]

Knowing that Eleutherius served as episcope during the years
174-189 C.E.[131], we can reasonably say that Irenaeus wrote his
work around the year 180 C.E.[132]

The whole work was written in Greek, but its complete text
has come down to us only in Latin. Opinions regarding the date
of this Latin translation vary from scholar to scholar.

> "According to H Jordan and A. Souter, it was performed
> in North Africa between 370 and 420. For H. Koch, it had
> to appear before 250, since it is used by Cyprian. V.
> Sanday goes back even further, since he assigns him the
> date of 200".[133]

---

[129] *Ibid.*

[130] Giorgio Maschio, Contro le eresie III,3,3, in *Op. cit.*, p. 219 (italics mine).

[131] DH 102.

[132] Cf. David T. Runia, Roberto Radice, *Op. cit.*, p. 123.

[133] Johannes Quasten, *Op. cit.,* pp. 258-259.

There are also numerous Greek fragments handed down from Hippolytus, Eusebius, and Epiphanius; an Armenian translation and other fragments into Syriac.[134]

Most critics agree that Irenaeus' "Against Heresies" is the first Christian work to mention infant baptism. The point-out step is as follows:

Omnes enim venit per semetipsum salvare: omnes, inquam, qui per eum renascuntur in Deum, infantes et parvulos et pueros et juvenes et seniores.[135]	In fact, he came to save everyone through his person: all, I say, those who through him are reborn in God, infants and children, young and old people.[136]

The text states that "all [...] are reborn in God". Irenaeus seems to have no doubts in speaking of the spiritual rebirth of children as well. Therefore the theologian Benedetto Testa[137] affirms:

> "[...] clear is the testimony of Irenaeus of Lyons who refers to the baptism conferred on children to reaffirm how Jesus saved everyone through his work".[138]

---

[134] For an exhaustive examination of all the numerous witnesses, I would recommend: John J. Dillon, *St. Irenaeus of Lyons against the heresies* (New York: Newman Press, 1992).

[135] *Adversus haereses*, a cura di Adelin Rousseau/Louis Doutreleau (Sources chrétiennes, 294), CERF, Parigi 1982, II,22,4, p. 220.

[136] Vittorino Dellagiacoma, *Contro le eresie* II,22,4, in *Op. Cit.*, p. 183.

[137] Full Professor of Dogmatic and Sacramental Theology at the Theological Institute of Ancona, adjunct to the Pontifical Lateran University and Professor at the Faculty of Theology of Lugano.

[138] Benedetto Testa, *I sacramenti della chiesa* (Milano: Jaca Book, 2007), p. 155.

The patristic scholar, Quasten, in his work already cited, states:

"[…] Irenaeus, is the first of ancient Christian literature to testify about the baptism of children […]".[139]

Despite similar apodictic statements, Kurt Aland offers a decidedly different reading. He brings attention to the sentences that precede the one in question:

"Coming to baptism at thirty years old, the perfect age to be a teacher, he came to Jerusalem to hear the deserved: Master! He was no different from what he appeared to be just as those who affirm when describing him that he appeared as he really was. Being a True teacher, therefore, he was of the age of a teacher, not denying or surpassing humanity, not transgressing the Law of mankind in himself, but sanctifying every age through assimilation to himself".[140]

And then on the sentences that follow:

"He passed through all ages, an infant to sanctify infants, a child to sanctify those who were of this age, at the same time being made for them a model of piety, justice and subjection; a youth for young people, their model, consecrating them to the Lord. So also an old person for the old, a perfect teacher in everything, not only in terms of the exposition of the truth but also in terms of age, sanctifying even the old, making himself their model […]".[141]

---

[139] Johannes Quasten, *Op.Cit.*, p. 278.
[140] Vittorino Dellagiacoma, Contro le eresie II,22,4, in *Op. cit.*, p. 183.
[141] *Ibidem.*

According to Aland, Irenaeus is arguing that Jesus, having presented himself at baptism at the very age to become a teacher, could sanctify everyone through "assimilation to himself", "becoming their model", that is, becoming a "model of piety", both for children and for adults.
His conclusion is as follows:

> "It does not seem apparent to me that Irenaeus has baptism in view here, and certainly there is no thought of infant baptism; he is concerned solely with the fact that Jesus sanctified all humanity in that he was made like all, lived through all ages of life and was an example to all [...]".[142]

Of course, Aland isn't the only one who thinks this way. The work edited by Giorgio Maschio makes no mention of baptism but merely comments in the following way:

> "[...] the idea that Jesus Christ is the perfect teacher because he not only communicated the truth but was an example in living it for all ages of human life shines through clearly".[143]

However, it must be honestly noted that the context is centred on the event of Christ's baptism and that the reference to the "rebirth in God" of children cannot exclude that Irenaeus was referring to their baptism without clearly exposing its practice. The passage is therefore to be considered ambiguous: neither of the two arguments (against or pro-paedobaptism) seems to have sufficient argumentative weight to prevail over the other.

---

[142] Kurt Aland, *Op. cit.*, p. 59.
[143] Giorgio Maschio, *Op. cit.*, p. 591, ftn. 2.

The transition to paedobaptism

If Tertullian, as we will see later, around 200 C.E. attests to the existence of a widespread trend in practising the baptism of children within Christianity, it is not at all impossible that twenty years earlier, in 180 C.E., Irenaeus witnessed the birth of that trend. If this were the case, from 180 to 200 C.E. the pro-paedobaptism arguments would have developed and spread within the communities.

If it were possible to trace some event that occurred close to the year 180 C.E. of adequate magnitude so as to offer a scenario compatible with a polarization of theological discussions regarding infant baptism, then we could historically corroborate the reading of Irenaeus offered by Benedetto Testa and most theologians. We know that around 165 C.E., during the reign of Marcus Aurelius, the Roman Empire was hit by what is called the first devastating epidemic, the so-called "Antonine Plague".

> "Some historians suspect that this was the first appearance of smallpox in the West. The disease was fatal, however. It lasted fifteen years, a quarter or a third of the population of the Empire died, including Marcus Aurelius himself, in 180 in Vienna".[144]

Mortality was so high that it was not unusual to see caravans of chariots coming out of the cities entirely loaded with the dead.

Dorothy Crawford, in her *Deadly Companions: How Microbes Shaped Our History*, writes that

> "[The] origin of the Antonine Plague was probably the city of Seleucia on the Tigris River near modern

---

[144] Rodney Stark, *Op. cit.*, p. 105.

Baghdad. Roman troops sent to calm a revolt plundered and plundered the city and returned triumphantly, spreading the plague along the way and bringing it home to Rome, where at its peak it killed around 5,000 people a day. It eventually spread throughout the empire reaching India and China".[145]

Her conclusions on the drama of the event are as follows:

"The Antonine Plague caused such a disastrous decline in population that the Roman Empire, worried about the workforce [needed] for all its functions, began to sink".[146]

As Rodney Stark well explains in his aforementioned work, Christians managed to face and overcome the epidemic more successfully than pagans. It can be hypothesized that the organization of Christian communities and the care that individual members showed towards the sick contributed to their lower mortality rate. But they certainly were not exempt from such a disaster. The same opinion is expressed by William H. McNeill

"One of the advantages that Christians enjoyed over their pagan contemporaries was that caring for the sick, even in times of pestilence, was considered a religious duty that they accepted. When all normal services become ineffective, even elementary care can greatly reduce mortality. Simply providing food and water, for example, allowed people temporarily too weak to care for themselves to recover rather than die miserably. Moreover, those who had survived through the assistance of others were likely to feel a sense of gratitude and intense

---

[145] Doroty H. Crawford, *Deadly Companions: How Microbes Shaped Our History* (Oxford: Oxford University Press, 2007), p. 78.
[146] *Ibid.*, p. 79.

solidarity with their rescuers. The effect of the disastrous epidemics, therefore, was to strengthen Christian communities at a time when many other institutions were falling into disrepute".[147]

From 165 to 180 C.E., one in three people died and undoubtedly, even among Christians, the most deaths occurred among the elderly and *children*.

"A quarter to a third of the entire population is believed to have died in the affected places. Since it is unlikely that such a disease would reach every inhabited area, the population of the empire as a whole did not decrease very significantly; however, the overall losses were considerable [...] In the years between 251 and 266, a new series of diseases of a magnitude comparable to the Antonine Plague of 165-180 struck the Roman world. [...] there are some significant circumstances on the basis of which we are tempted to believe that these two demographic disasters were indicative of the arrival and progressive development among Mediterranean populations of two of the most fearsome childhood diseases with which we are familiar, namely measles and smallpox".[148]

Although there is no unanimity on the actual scale of the tragedy, we can say that it had a considerable impact. According to Prof. Elio Lo Cascio[149]

"[in] limited areas of Egypt, the depopulation attributable to the epidemic led to a decrease of more than 90% of the

---

[147] William Hardy McNeill, *La peste nella storia* (Milano: Res Gestae, 2012), p. 109.
[148] William Hardy McNeill, *op. cit.*, p. 109.
[149] Full Professor of Roman History at the University of Naples "Federico II".

total population. The estimates - in the order of 14-20% - of the number of victims of the pandemic in relation to the total population of the empire, advanced by R.J. Littman [...] are probably to be considered too low [...]"[150].

And it was precisely in second-century Egypt that, according to some scholars, the first baptisms of children took place. Fausto Salvoni[151], for example, writes:

"[children] began to [be baptized] in Egypt in the second century; from this region, the use then passed to other districts arousing at the beginning not a few oppositions".[152]

As history has recorded several times, crises triggered by natural disasters, war or otherwise, have often resulted in crises of faith. That catastrophes generate religious responses is the orthodoxy of historical sociology. My hypothesis is that, once the epidemic ended in 180 C.E., Irenaeus and the other Christian theologians directed, as never before, their reflections on God's salvific will towards children. Reflections that gave an impulse to the development of a theology of infant baptism and a push to spread its teaching in the following twenty years, so much so that Tertullian, at the dawn of the third century, speaks of it as a too lightly accepted practice. Twenty years do not seem at all excessive for a theological elaboration of paedobaptism and for a diffusion of this practice in the various churches.

---

[150] Cited by Eliodoro Savino in *Campania tardo antica (284-604 d.C.)* (Bari: Edipuglia, 2005), ftn. 311.

[151] The theologian and Professor Fausto Salvoni (1907-1982) collaborated in the compilation of the first three volumes of the Catholic Encyclopedia and in the preparation of the famous Concordat Bible, 1968 edition.

[152] Fausto Salvoni, *Il battesimo* (Genova: Editrice Lanterna, 1976), p. 81.

I consider it probable that the Antonine Plague has "polarized" these theological reflections. By polarization, I mean precisely the technical term that the psychosocial sciences apply to group dynamics, that is:

> "[…] the shift and extremization of individual opinions, following a group discussion, in the direction already preferred before the discussion".[153]

Dr Massimo Introvigne, a well-known sociologist of religions, commented:

> "The hypothesis is suggestive and seems to open a relevant track, in my opinion, especially on the first part (God's salvific will towards children), while for baptism, there were probably also factors that relate - to use Lakatos's distinction - to the "internal history" of theology as well as to its "external history". The two histories, however, always influence each other".[154]

Among the factors "pertaining to internal history" it is likely that numerical growth is to be included. It should be remembered that according to Stark[155], the most plausible estimate of the actual growth rate of Christianity in the first two centuries calculates a number of Christians exceeding 100,000 people in 180 C.E. In addition to external proselytism, it is clear that internal growth and the presence of increasingly numerous children may have contributed to theological discussions on infant baptism.

---

[153] Alberto Voci, *Processi psicosociali nei gruppi* (Bari: Editori Laterza, 2003), p. 75.

[154] Private correspondence, by e-mail, authorized for publication.

[155] Rodney Stark, *Op. Cit.*, p. 18.

On baptism by Tertullian

Quintus Septimius Florent Tertullian was born in Carthage to rather wealthy pagan parents who allowed him to receive a first-rate cultural education. His art of writing and stylistic mastery is an undisputed talent that has made him the apologist *par excellence*. His works can be divided into three groups:

- Apologetic works: *Ad nationes, Apologeticum, De testimonio animae, Ad scapulam, Adversus Iudaeos.*
- Anti-heretical works: *De praescriptione haereticorum, Adversus Marcionem, Adversus Hermogenem, Adversus Valentinianos, De baptismo, De carne Christi, De resurrectione carnis, Adversus Praxean, De anima.*
- Ethical-disciplinary works: *Ad martyras, De spectaculis, De cultu feminarum, De oratione, De patientia, De paenitentia, Aduxorem, De exhortatione castitatis, De monogamia, De virginibus velandis, De corona, De fuga in persecuzione, De idolatria, De ieiuno adversus psychicos, De pudicitia, De pallio.*

The list of these works, and the topics he addressed, show the figure and depth of his argumentative sophistication. I don't think you can use better words than those used by Quasten to describe the figure:

> "To a deep knowledge of Greek and Latin philosophy, law and literature, he combines inexhaustible vigor, inflamed rhetoric and biting satire. He is not a man of compromise. Always in the breach, no respite is given in the struggle he sustains against the adversary, whether it be the pagans, the Jews, the heretics, or, later, the

Catholics themselves".[156]

Unfortunately, even Tertullian's biography is basically unknown to us. A useful clue is provided by Jerome in his *De viris illustribus*:

> "The Tertullian priest ... a native of Africa and precisely of Carthage, son of a proconsular centurion, of acute ingenuity and impetuous character, he flourished under the emperors Severus and Antoninus Caracalla. He wrote many works, which we do not list here, because they are well known ... Tertullian was a priest of the Church until the age of forty; then, due to the envy and insults from the clergy of the Church of Rome, he gravitated the Montanist heresy ... It is said that he lived to a very late age and that he also published other works, now lost".[157]

Jerome informs us that at the age of about forty, Tertullian devotes himself to the heretical ideas of Montano[158]. The first traces of Montanist ideas are found in his work *Adversus Marcionem*; since the first book of this work refers to the fifteenth year of Severus, that is, 207 C.E., it is assumed that the

---

[156] Johannes Quasten, *Op. Cit.*, p. 493.

[157] Claudio Moreschini, Luigi Rusca, *Apologia del cristianesimo, La carne di Cristo* (Milano: Biblioteca Universale Rizzoli, 2000), p. 67.

[158] "At its origins, Montanism, so called by Montano, the Phrygian prophet who together with two women, Priscilla and Massimilla, with his ecstatic preaching gave life to the movement in the central regions of Asia Minor (Lydia and Phrygia), is essentially a revival of the prophetic charism, a revival of apocalyptic enthusiasm. In fact, it presents itself as a "new prophecy", therefore a new revelation of a prophetic character, in which Jesus' promise to send the Paraclete contained in the fourth Gospel is fulfilled and which, taking its cue from the heavenly Jerusalem prophesied by the Johannine Apocalypse, proclaims the imminent end of the world and invites his followers to gather in a particular place (the valley of Pepuza) in expectation of this end." - Giorgio Jossa, *Op. Cit.*, p. 121.

conversion took place shortly before that date. If so, according to what Jerome says, Tertullian was born about forty years earlier, that is, around 160 CE[159]. Having lived to a "very late age", he is thought to have died around 230 C.E. In fact

> "the *De pudicitia* seems to be his last work, composed under the episcopate of Callisto (but even this news is controversial) that is between 217-8 and 222-3".[160]

Tertullian is the first Christian author of the second century to unequivocally mention infant baptism. He does so in his work entitled *De baptismo*. Regarding the date of composition,

> "Certainly, it should be traced back to the "Catholic" period of the author, since in the treatise there is no trace of references to Montanism: most scholars place the work in the years 200-206".[161]

Other scholars propose a slightly high date, that is, between 198 and 200 C.E.[162]

According to the scheme provided by Matteoli, the *De baptismo* is divided into three main parts:

- Chapters 1 through 9: the author responds to the criticisms of the heretics and explains some parts of the baptismal rite.
- Chapters 10-16: Tertullian shows that there is one and only one baptism.

---

[159] Claudio Moreschini, Luigi Rusca, *Op. Cit.*, p. 68.
[160] *Ibidem.*
[161] Sara Matteoli, *De baptismo, introduzione*, in Sandra Isetta, Sara Matteoli, Teresa Piscitelli, Valentina Sturli, *Tertulliano, opere catechetiche* (Roma: Città Nuova Editrice, 2008), p. 154.
[162] Johannes Quasten, *Op. Cit.*, p. 522.

-    Chapters 17-20: set forth a series of practical rules for the administration of baptism, which is not to be granted lightly.

How has this work been transmitted to us?

> "It appears for the first time in Mesnar's edition of 1545 (B): he based his work on a lost manuscript of the ninth century, related, it seems, to the Codex Agobardinus [...] For his edition of 1550, however, Sigismund Ghelen used, in addition to Mesnart's edition, another manuscript, the Codex Masburensis, also lost [...] In 1916 A. Wilmart discovered a codex of the twelfth century of the library of Clairvaux, now in Troyes, containing five treatises of Tertullian, including the Bapt".[163]

As mentioned earlier, this writing, composed at the beginning of the third century in response to the heresy of the Cainites[164], is the first clear historical document to mention the use of imparting baptism to infants.

At the beginning of chapter 18, Tertullian manifests one of his main concerns:

Ceterum baptismum non temere credendum esse sciunt quorum	Those charged with administering baptism know that it is not to be

---

[163] Sara Matteoli, *Op. Cit.*, p. 157.

[164] "In the second century C.E. the Cainites were one of the many sects within Gnosticism, but they never had great importance [...] The Cainites resumed, taking it to the extreme consequences, the opposition, typical of Gnosticism, between the supreme God and the Creator God of the Old Testament [...] they rejected baptism, considering it unnecessary to obtain salvation [...]" – *Ibid.* p. 153.

| officium est.[165]

| given lightly. [166]

Given the importance of this sacrament, which for Tertullian marks a second birth, it must be granted with caution.
And here is the point:

itaque pro cuiusque personae condicione ac dispositione, etiam aetate, cunctatio baptismi utilior est, praecipue tamen circa parvulos. Quid enim necesse, si non tam necesse est, sponsores etiam periculo ingeri, qui et ipsi per mortalitatem destituere promissiones suas possunt et proventu malae indolis falli? Ait quidem Dominos: *Nolite illos prohibere ad me venire.* Veniant ergo, dum adolescunt, dum discunt, dum quo veniant docentur; fiant Christiani cum Christum nosse potuerint![167]

Therefore, according to each person's condition, disposition, and even age, it is preferable to delay baptism, especially when dealing with young children. What need is there, if there is no real need, to expose the godparents to the danger of breaking their promises in the event of death or of being disappointed by the development of an evil personality? Certainly, the Lord says, "Let the children come to me." But let them come when they are older, when they can learn, when the One toward whom they

---

[165] Sara Matteoli, Bapt. 18,1 in *Op. Cit.*, p. 190.
[166] *Ibid.*, p. 191.
[167] Bapt. 18,4-5, in *ibid.*, p. 190.

> are going is shown. Let
> them become
> Christians when they
> can know Christ![168]

Tertullian was clearly opposed to baptism being administered to children who were unable to fully understand the meaning of this rite. But it is equally clear that paedobaptism was already an established reality.

The fact that Tertullian mentions a passage from Matthew's gospel[169] and offers his own exegesis against infant baptism is extremely interesting. This seems to confirm how, in the years leading up to it, a paedobaptismal theology had been developed and spread that appealed to the authority of the gospels.

The mention of "godparents" and their vicarious responsibility is also an unequivocal sign of a liturgy already formulated and adopted in the communities. Interesting is also the reflection that Tertullian makes by contrasting the "necessity" of baptism with the concept of "innocens aeta":

Quid festinat innocens aetas ad remissionem peccatorum?[170]	Why is this innocent age rushing to receive the remission of sins?[171]

The question that needs to be asked is whether Tertullian was opposing the spread of an idea of original sin. Was the concept of "purity" that characterized child *status* very present in the

---

[168] *Ibid.*, p. 191.

[169] "but Jesus said, 'Let the children come to me, and do not stop them, for it is to such as these that the kingdom of heaven belongs'" – Matthew 19:14 (NRSVUE).

[170] Bapt. 18,5, in *ibid.*, pp. 190, 192.

[171] *Ibid.*, pp. 191,193.

Christian literature of the first half of the second century, diminishing to give more and more room for the "stain" of original sin? The confirmation seems to come later from Cyprian[172], also born in Carthage (like Tertullian) around 210 C.E.: to him, we owe, in fact, the original declaration which stated that the baptism of children procured the remission of original sin.[173]

All this supports the hypothesis that between the time of Irenaeus and that of Tertullian theological reflections developed which moved towards the baptism of infants.

Tertullian, however, shows himself in favour of a return to the old concept, from which he had probably never strayed. This conviction is also expressed in his other works, for example in *De anima*, where he states:

Hinc enim et apostolus ex sanctificato alterutro sexu sanctos procreari ait, tam ex seminis praerogativa quam ex institutionis disciplina. Ceterum, inquit, immundi nascerentur, quasi designatos tamen sanctitatis ac per hoc etiam salutis intellegi volens fidelium filios, ut huius spei pignore	For this reason, in fact, the apostle also affirms that from one of the two parents who has been sanctified, saints are born, both for their origin and for their education. "Otherwise - he continues - they would be born impure", as if he wanted it to be understood that the

---

[172] Cyprian (ca. 210-258) lived at the time of the second great plague which struck the Roman world about 70 years after the Antonine Plague and which took the name of "Plague of Cyprian". As we will see later, Cyprian's statements may be somewhat relevant to my hypothesis.

[173] McGrath, A.E., *Op. Cit.*, p. 517.

matrimoniis, quae retinenda censuerat, patrocinaretur.[174]

children of Christians are destined to purity and therefore also to salvation, to protect with the pledge of this hope the marriages that he had established to save.[175]

Tertullian's counter-current efforts will prove to be in vain, and the practice of paedobaptism will end up becoming firmly established in the following years, that is, at the time of Hippolytus.

---

[174] De anima 39,4, in Menghi, M. (a cura di), *Tertulliano, L'anima*, Marsilio Editori, Venezia 1988, pp. 164, 166.
[175] *Ibid.*, pp. 165,167.

We have thus reached approximately the year 215 C.E., the year around which "Hippolytus"[176] composed his *Apostolic Tradition*. But who was our author?

> "According to Photius (*Bibl. Cod. 121*), he himself declared himself, in one of the disappeared writings, a disciple of Irenaeus. If he was such, he certainly shared the master's zeal for the defence of Catholic doctrine against heresy".[177]

It is assumed that its origins were neither Roman nor Latin but Oriental. This conclusion has been reached because of "his surprising knowledge of Greek philosophy".[178] We know that he was a bishop, but we do not know exactly the seat of this episcopate. Eusebius informs us only that Hippolytus was "bishop of another Church in another region".[179] Opinions range from Rome to Porto and the Arab city of Bostra in present-day southern Syria.[180] According to the generally accepted thesis, he lived between 170 and 236 C.E.

Because of the disputes he had with Bishop Callistus, who succeeded Zephyrinus, Hippolytus is remembered as the first antipope in history. Callistus accused Hippolytus of being a ditheist, while Hippolytus accused Callistus of professing

---

[176] It is deserved to point out that the authorship of this work is not recognized by several scholars.

[177] Johannes Quasten, *Op. Cit.*, p. 421.

[178] *Ibidem.*

[179] Franzo Migliore, *Historia Ecclesiastica* VI.20 in *Op. Cit.*, p. 40.

[180] Cf. Rachele Tateo, *La tradizione apostolica* (Milano, Edizioni Paoline, 1995), p. 8 ftn. 4.

Sabellianism.[181]

> "When Pope Callistus mitigated discipline for penitents who had committed mortal sins, the austere and ambitious Hippolytus accused him of departing, with his softness, from the tradition of the early Church. And he also reproached him for being a disciple of Sabellius and a heretic, and with a number of partisans, he broke away from the Church. Elected bishop of Rome by a small but influential circle, he became one of the first antipopes".[182]

The schism lasted until 235 C.E., when both Hippolytus and Pontian, who succeeded Urban (who succeeded Callistus), were sent into exile in Sardinia by the emperor Maximinus Thrax. There, it seems that the two bishops were reconciled by renouncing each other's office. Both died in exile.

> "Pope Fabian (236-250) had their bodies brought back to Rome and solemnly buried them, Pope Pontian in the papal crypt of s. Callisto, and Ippolito in the cemetery of Via Tiburtina, which still bears his name".[183]

In 1973, under the basilica of the Sacred Island near Fiumicino, a sarcophagus was discovered that is thought to contain the relics of Hippolytus, probably transferred there by Bishop Formoso, who later became pope in 891 C.E. All this would be proven by a slab of white marble found inside the sarcophagus and bearing the inscription[184]:

---

[181] "Term indicating an early Christological heresy, which considered the three persons of the Trinity to be different historical manifestations of the only one God", see McGrath, A., *Op. Cit.*, p. 577.

[182] Johannes Quasten, *Op. Cit.*, pp. 421-422.

[183] Johannes Quasten, *Op. Cit.*, p. 422.

[184] Danilo Mazzoleni, *I reperti epigrafici* (Roma: Viella Libreria Editrice, 1983), p. 135.

+ hic requi

Escit bea

Tus Ypoli

Tus mar(tyr)

Although the attribution of the *Apostolic Tradition* (written around 215 C.E.) to Hippolytus of Rome has come under well founded criticism, it is undoubtedly the most important testimony on the life and liturgy of the early Christian community, after the Didache.

There are numerous translations in Latin, Coptic, Arabic and Ethiopian.

"The Latin version, probably dating from the IV century, was discovered on a palimpsest dating from the last quarter of the V century in the library of the Verona Cathedral Chapter [...] Unfortunately, it only includes part of the work".[185]

However, we can be sure that we have a reliable text available, and we owe this to the research carried out independently by two scholars, E. Schwartz and R.H. Connolly, who both identified the work with the Constitution of the Egyptian Church, preserved in the Alexandrian Synod.[186]

In addition to these two testimonies, three adaptations of the text[187] have been identified:

- Book VIII of *Apostolic Constitutions* (an extensive liturgical-canonical collection dating back to no earlier

---

[185] Johannes Quasten, *Op. Cit.*, p. 438.
[186] Cf. Rachele Tateo, *Op. Cit.*, p. 23 ftn. 3.
[187] *Ibid.*, p. 24,25.

than the sixth century).

- *Testament of Our Lord* (dated to the fifth century that has among its sources an apocryphal gospel).
- *Canons of Hippolytus* (a reworking of the *Apostolic Tradition*, born in an Egyptian environment and datable to the middle of the fourth century).

The work is structured in three main parts.

"The first contains a prologue, canons on the election and consecration of a bishop, the prayer of his consecration, the Eucharistic liturgy that follows this ceremony, and the blessings of oil, cheese and olives".[188]

"[...] the second legislates for the laity. It contains regulations affecting new converts, arts and professions forbidden to Christians, catechumens, baptism, confirmation and first communion".[189]

"The third part of the Apostolic Tradition deals with different Christian practices. He gives a description of the Sunday Eucharist. There are rules on fasting, agape and the oil blessing ceremony. [...] Regulations for burial, morning prayer and catechetical teaching follow".[190]

The second part contains unequivocal indications relating to the baptism of infants. In it, we read:

"At the crowing of the rooster, first pray on the water. Whether water flowing into a spring or flowing from above. That is how it happens unless there is some need.

---

[188] Johannes Quasten, *Op. Cit.*, pp. 442-443.
[189] *Ibid.*, p. 446.
[190] *Ibid.*, p. 448.

> If there is a permanent and urgent need, use the water you
> find. (Those who are to receive baptism) undress. Baptize
> children first. All those who are able to respond by
> themselves, answer; for those who are not able, answer
> the parents or someone from the family".[191]

Not only did it mention, without a shadow of a doubt, that
children had to be baptized, but it is also specified that, for those
children who were too young and therefore unable to answer
baptismal questions, parents or godparents should answer on
their behalf. They were then baptized in *fide aliena*.

It is possible that these instructions are the result of a
theological evolution that takes its cue from the baptismal
theology that already existed, albeit sketchily, in that passage
previously defined as "ambiguous" in *Against Heresies*,
examined above.[192]

Aland insinuates the doubt that the whole section is, in fact,
a later interpolation.[193] But, as he himself later acknowledges, it
is a doubt that does not rest on any concrete basis. Although
Apostolic Tradition does not affirm at any point that
paedobaptism is to be considered obligatory[194], it is undeniably
documented in its unequivocal liturgical formulation.

---

[191] Rachele Tateo, *Op. Cit.*, pp. 80-81.
[192] See p. 59.
[193] Kurt Aland, *Op. Cit.*, pp. 49-50.
[194] The habit of being baptized as an adult still remained in place for several
centuries.

Conclusion

The temptation to "bend" History to Theology is no less strong than that one who would like to see Theology depending on historical events alone. It is very easy for a historian, especially of Christianity, to make the mistake of crossing the limit that separates his professional figure from that of a theologian. This limit is called "judgment". Marc Bloch, the father of modern historical methodology, said that

> "Past was so actively used to explain the Present with the intention of justifying it or condemning it better. So that, in many cases, the demon of the origins was perhaps only a disguise of this other diabolical enemy of the real history: the mania of judgment".[195]

In the exposition of the Christian documents that we have analyzed, I have tried, as far as I could, to avoid any form of theological judgment on the events narrated. Following the "invitation" of Bloch, I tried to suggest what I would call a simple "working hypothesis" that could open a "relevant track" for subsequent insights.

> "Human facts are, by essence, very delicate phenomena, and many of them escape mathematical calculation. [...] Where it is impossible to calculate, it is necessary *to suggest*".[196]

So, here is my "suggestion".

---

[195] Marc Bloch, *Apologia della storia* (Torino: Einaudi editore, 1998), p. 27.
[196] Marc Bloch, *Op. Cit.*, p. 23 (*italics added*).

According to Stark[197], Christianity would likely have grown at a rate of 40% per decade; according to his estimates, the number of Christians would have exceeded 215,000 by the year 200 C.E. It is clear that the increasing presence of children within Christian communities began to constitute a "problem" for theologians to ponder.

The Antonine Plague, which struck the Roman Empire between 165 and 180 C.E., was interpreted both by the Romans and the Christians in a religious key.

Regarding the Romans,

> "Marcus Aurelius brought in priests from all over and also favoured the acceptance of all forms of prayer and rituals. The emperor held the belief that the plague was the result of divine wrath and observed (perhaps even personally) a variety of religious, Roman and foreign rituals with purifying purposes".[198]

---

[197] Rodney Stark, *Op. cit.*, p. 17.

[198] Sergio Sabbatani and Sirio Fiorino (2019) "The Antonine Plague and the decline of the Roman Empire. The role of the Parthian and Marcomanni Wars between 164 and 182 AD in spreading contagion", *Le Infezioni in Medicina*, n.4, pp. 261-274.

LITERARY EVIDENCE ON PAEDOBAPTISM

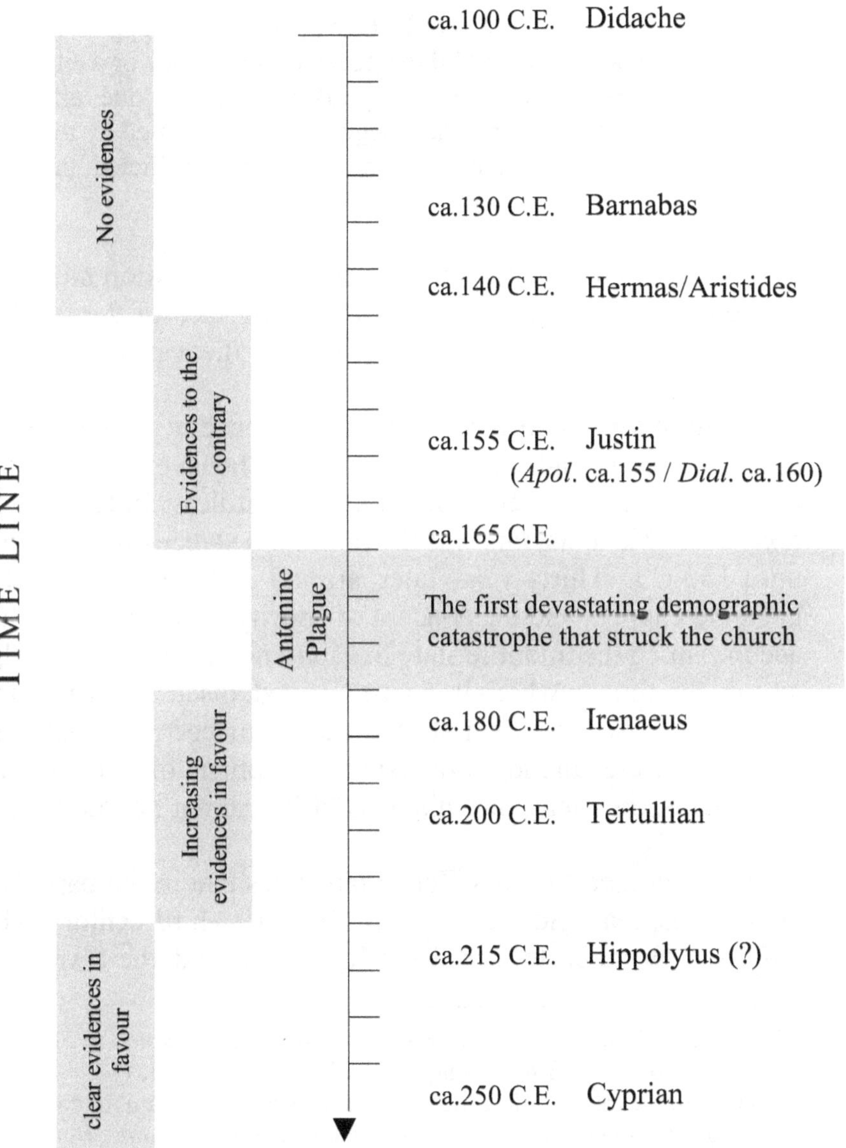

Conclusion

That period coincided with a resurgence of persecutory activity against Christians.

> "In the eyes of these people, Christians were to appear as those who had disturbed the peace of a province or a city by taking away from the gods the honors due and unleashing, in return, their anger, as demonstrated by the various plagues, natural and social, that afflicted the empire".[199]

Concerning the Christians, religious interpretation must have influenced their thought, especially in the face of the death of children and young people born within the various ecclesial communities.

In summary, there is no explicit reference to infant baptism during the entire sub-Apostolic period. Whenever the subject is broached, infants are considered pure regardless. Judging by the texts available to us, this was the dominant stance on this subject until 150 C.E. Thirty years later, around 180 C.E., the situation began to change, and the concept of "purity" that had, until then, accompanied the infantile state began to be lost. Could it be that, around the time in which Irenaeus[200] lived, discussions about the practice of paedobaptism started taking place? And that some *ecclesiae* were already practising a baptism of infants? The documents are silent, but this possibility cannot be totally ruled out.

After another 20 years, Tertullian states that infant baptism is now widespread. So we arrive in the early third century when the last resistance to Tertullian has fallen and the "Apostolic

---

[199] Giovanni Filoramo, *Alla ricerca di un'identità cristiana*, in *Storia del Cristianesimo, L'antichità* (Roma: Editori Laterza, 2001), p. 171.

[200] The first explicit reference to infant baptism (although considered ambiguous by some scholar) is the one we can read in *Against Heresies* by Irenaeus, ca. 180 C.E. See p. 65 ff.

Tradition" describes the practice of paedobaptism and its regulation such as to suggest that it was accepted without reservation by the Christian world of that time.

It follows that, between 150 and 180 C.E., something must have happened to justify such a major change on a subject that lies at the heart of Christian life. The Antonine Plague fits perfectly in the history of baptismal theology, presenting itself as a crucial event on the world stage.

The problem with this scenario is that the connection between the beginnings of infant baptism and the Antonine Plague is purely hypothetical because no literary source explicitly expresses it. I have already had the opportunity to point out that

> "not only is the link between the plague and the infant baptism missing, but also any type of generic mention of the plague in the writings of contemporary Christian authors".[201]

So why this silence? To answer this question, we can try to get some insights from Cyprian who, writing about the plague that broke out 70 years later, stated

> "Indeed, a certain dismay assails some Christians at the fact that the spread of this disease touches our brethren as well as the Gentiles. The Christian would almost tend to believe that he must go free from the contagion of evils and happily enjoy the century in order to be predestined to future glory without having to endure all the adverse trials in this life. Therefore, dismay assails those Christians who are disturbed by the fact that this common mortality touches them together with the pagans (VIII) [...] He who, not reborn of water and the spirit, is condemned to Geena

---

[201] Arduini, F. (2021). Epistles: The Pandemic Origins of Child Baptism. *Biblical Archaeology Review*, 47(1), pp. 70–71.

> (XIV) [...] Many of our loved ones die because of the pestilence, that is, they are freed from the snares of the century. (XV) [...] Children avoid the risk of puberty, but happily attain the prize of continence and innocence. (XV)".[202]

If Christians were assailed by dismay at the time of Cyprian, 70 years after the Antonine Plague, surely they would be more shocked by the very first catastrophe that stroke the Church! Looking at the time of the Antonine Plague through Cyprian's eyes, we can say that Christians -still living in the imminence of Christ's return- were much more convinced that they "go free from the contagion" and that the plague would only affect the Gentiles.

So, the apologists had to face a sort of theological disorientation: how to justify this awful plague, which was considered a "sign of divine punishment" by the pagan population? Moreover, we can also assume that every learned debate was silenced by the emergency of the epidemic. The plausible demands for seriously ill children by their Christian parents, who wanted to ensure their salvation through baptism, needed immediate action. That's why it was only when the calamity ended, around 180 C.E., that the first references began to appear.

The silence of the sources[203] is a problem that is bound to remain open, but it cannot be ignored that it can be interpreted

---

[202] *De mortalitate* VIII, XIV, XV in Mario Ruggero, (ed) *Poesia e teologia della morte* (Roma: Città Nuova Editrice, 1997), pp. 26, 27, 32. See also Cyprian, *Epistle* 64: VI,2.

[203] I wonder if this Christian sources' silence can somehow be included in the scenario of crisis in record-keeping during Antonine Plague described by Richard Duncan-Jones. See Richard Duncan-Jones (1991), The impact of Antonine plague, *Journal of Roman Archaeology*, pp. 108-139. See also Richard Duncan-Jones (2018), *Arctos* n.52, pp. 41-72.

within the coherence framework presented by my hypothesis:

> *the theological development of the practice of infant baptism received a decisive impulse from the demographic catastrophe generated by the Antonine Plague.*

Postface

It was the year 2009 when I first decided to make public my hypothesis on the possible relationship between the origins of paedobaptism and the Antonine Plague. I did so through a short book[204] available in Italian, now here updated and translated into English. Honestly, in Italy, my hypothesis has not received the attention I would have expected. Although it is sad to say, I live in a country where any topic that is antithetical to the religious sensibilities of the Catholic mainstream struggles to find space for discussion. With rare exceptions expressed privately, in the ten years since, no one has ever publicly mentioned my hypothesis, not even relegating it to some brief marginal note.

Then, ten years later, what nobody would have ever imagined happened: the whole world experienced its first modern pandemic (Covid19), and everything changed.

Italy, my country, was one of the most heavily afflicted. Newspapers headlined the Italian situation using words like "tragedy"[205], "disaster"[206], and so on.

Italian doctors had to choose who died and who lived due to the lack of hospital resources. I have personally seen lines of army trucks loaded with coffins leaving the city of Bergamo[207] (the epicentre of the first wave of coronavirus) less than an hour's drive from my home. As I experienced these moments,

---

[204] Francesco Arduini, *Il battesimo dei bambini. Un'ipotesi sulle origini* (Roma: Aracne editrice, 2010).

[205] https://www.bbc.com/news/world-europe-52067673.

[206] https://www.latimes.com/world-nation/story/2020-04-26/perfect-storm-virus-disaster-in-italys-lombardy-region-is-a-lesson-for-the-world.

[207] https://www.reuters.com/article/health-coronavirus-italy-idINKBN2161FL.

the images before my eyes were overlaid with the catastrophic images of the Antonine Plague that I had mentally constructed during my past historical research. So, while the news showed long lines of trucks carrying the dead to the cemetery, in my mind, I saw them as "caravans of chariots coming out of the Roman empire's cities entirely loaded with the dead".

A sight one can hardly forget. Nevertheless, all of us have suffered to a greater or lesser degree and perhaps lost some loved ones in this tragedy.

The pandemic of Covid19 has disrupted the most established religious traditions and rituals in history, too. *IlSole24Ore*, one of the most renowned newspapers in Italy, well described what happened in an article titled "Coronavirus, how the Church reinvented itself not to disappear during the lockdown":

> "All masses are suspended, the celebration of every sacrament as well: the Church is moving towards Easter as never before in its recent history. The climax of the liturgical year and of Christian life will be celebrated behind closed doors, without the presence of the faithful, as never before, wartime included". [208]

The fact that the Church, during this modern pandemic, profoundly modified what had been an unchanged orthopraxis for centuries removed any doubt from my mind that, *mutatis mutandis*, the early Church also had to react to the pandemic by modifying what was the practice of that time, specifically by introducing baptism to ensure the salvation of the affected children.

Unfortunately, we have had the opportunity to see how a pandemic is able to change the habits of every population.

---

[208] https://www.ilsole24ore.com/art/coronavirus-cosi-chiesa-si-e-reinventata-non-scomparire-il-lockdown-ADLWDKJ.

During this period, my hypothesis began to attract the interest of some magazines, including the *Biblical Archaeology Review*[209], *Post Augustum Journal*[210], and others.

While I hope that any residual effects of this modern pandemic will disappear completely in the shortest possible time, I hope that my hypothesis will continue to be debated and deepened by attracting the interest of more and more scholars.

Francesco Arduini

---

[209] https://www.baslibrary.org/biblical-archaeology-review/47/1/24.
[210] http://www.postaugustum.com/journal/οι-πανδημικές-καταβολές-του-νηπιοβαπ-2/.

Abbreviations

Apol.	Apologies of Justin Martyr
Ar.	Apology of Aristides of Athens
Bapt.	On baptism by Tertullian
Barn.	Letter of Barnabas
ca.	*Circa* (about)
cf.	*Confer* (compare)
DH	*Enchiridion symbolorum, definitionum et declarationum de rebus fidei et morum*
Dial.	Dialogue with Tryphon by Justin Martyr
Did.	Didache
ed.	Editor(s)
et al.	*Et alia* (and others)
ff.	And following pages
NA28	Nestle-Aland *Novum Testamentum Graece*, 28th edition
NRSVUE	New Revised Standard Version Updated Edition
Op. Cit.	*Opere citato* (cited work)

Bibliography

ALAND, K., *Did the early church baptize infants?*, Wipf and Stock, Oregon 2004.

ALPIGIANO, C. (ed.), *Aristide di Atene. Apologia*, Nardini editore, Firenze 1988.

BARTH, G., *Il battesimo in epoca protocristiana*, Paideia Editrice, Brescia 1987.

BARTH, K., *Il fondamento della vita cristiana*, Casa Editrice Battista, Roma 1976.

BLOCH, M., *Apologia della storia*, Einaudi editore, Torino 1998.

BUONAIUTI, C.M. (ed.), *Storia del Cristianesimo*, Newton&Compton editori, Roma 2002.

CARANDINI, A., *Antonino Pio e Marco Aurelio*, Rizzoli, Milano 2021.

CIVEA, S. and MOSCATELLI, F. (eds.), *Didaché: Dottrina dei Dodici Apostoli*, Edizioni San Paolo, Cinisello Balsamo 1999.

CLERICI, A. (ed.), *Didaché. Lettere di Ignazio d'Antiochia. A Diogneto*, Ediz. Paoline, Milano 2002.

CORSANI, B., *I vangeli sinottici*, Claudiana, Torino 2008.

CRAWFORD, D.H., *Deadly Companions: How Microbes Shaped Our History*, Oxford University Press, Oxford 2007.

CULLMANN, O., *Die Tauflehre des Neuen Testaments*, Zwingli-Verlag, Zürich 1948.

DELLAGIACOMA, P.V. (ed.), *Contro le eresie*, vol. I, Edizioni Cantagalli, Siena 1996.

DILLON, J. (ed.), *St. Irenaeus of Lyons against the heresies*, Newman Press, New York 1992.

DROBNER, H., *Patrologia*, Piemme, Casale Monferrato 2002.

EHRMAN, B.D., *Lost Scriptures, Books That Did Not Make It Into The New Testament*, Oxford University Press, New York

2003.

FERRARIO, F., *Libertà di credere*, Claudiana, Torino 2000.

FILORAMO, G. and MENOZZI, D. (eds.), *Storia del Cristianesimo, L'antichità*, Editori Laterza, Roma 2001.

GIRGENTI, G. (ed.), *Giustino – Apologie*, Rusconi Libri, Milano 1995.

HAHNEMAN, G.M., *The Muratorian Fragment and the Development of the Canon*, Oxford University Press, Oxford 1992.

HARRIS, J.R. and ROBINSON, J.R. (eds.), *The apology of Aristides on behalf of the Christians*, University Press, Cambridge 1893.

ISETTA, S. (ed.), *Tertulliano, opere catechetiche*, Città Nuova Editrice, Roma 2008.

JOSSA, G., *Il cristianesimo antico. Dalle origini al concilio di Nicea*, Carocci editore, Roma 2007.

LO BUE, F. (ed.), *Il catechismo di Heidelberg (1563)*, edizione Gioventù cristiana, Torre Pellice 1939.

LO CASCIO, E. (ed.), *L'impatto della "peste antonina"*, Edipuglia, Bari 2012.

MASCHIO, G. (ed.), *Contro le eresie e gli altri scritti*, Jaca Book, Milano 1997.

MAZZOLENI, D., *I reperti epigrafici*, Viella Libreria editrice, Roma 1983.

McGRATH, A., *Teologia cristiana*, Claudiana, Torino 2003.

MENGHI, M. (ed.), *Tertulliano, L'anima*, Marsilio Editori, Venezia 1988.

MIGLIORE, F. (ed.), *Eusebio di Cesarea, storia ecclesiastica/1*, Città Nuova Editrice, Roma 2005.

MIEGGE, G., *Il battesimo dei fanciulli, nella storia, nella teoria, nella prassi*, Claudiana Editrice, Torre Pelice 1943.

MORESCHINI, C. and RUSCA, L. (eds.), *Apologia del cristianesimo, La carne di Cristo*, Biblioteca Universale

Rizzoli, Milano 2000.

PENNA, R. (ed.), *Le origini del cristianesimo*, Ediz. Carocci, Roma 2004.

POUDERON, B. (*et al.*), *Apologie*, (source chrétiennes, 470), CERF, Parigi 2003.

QUACQUARELLI, A. (ed.), *Il pastore di Erma*, Città Nuova Editrice, Roma 2007.

QUASTEN, J., *Patrologia. I primi due secoli (II-III)*, Marietti editore, Casale 1980.

RICCA, P., *Dal battesimo allo "sbattezzo"*, Claudiana Editrice, Torino 2015.

ROUSSEAU A. and DOUTRELEAU, L. (eds.), *Adversus haereses*, (Sources chrétiennes, 294), CERF, Parigi 1982.

RUNIA, D. and RADICE, R. (eds.) *Filone di Alessandria nella prima letteratura cristiana*, Vita e Pensiero, Milano 1999.

SALVONI, F., *Il battesimo*, Editrice Lanterna, Genova 1976.

SAVINO, E., *Campania tardo antica (284-604 d.C.)*, Edipuglia, Bari 2005.

SCORZA BARCELLONA, F., *Epistola di Barnaba*, Società Editrice Internazionale, Torino 1975.

SHARPE, S. (ed.), *The Epistle of Barnabas from the sinaitic manuscript of the Bible*, Williams and Norgate, Londra 1880.

STARK, R., *Ascesa e affermazione del cristianesimo*, Lindau, Torino 2007.

TATEO, R. (ed.), *La tradizione apostolica*, Edizioni Paoline, Milano 1995.

TESTA, B., *I sacramenti della chiesa*, Jaca Book, Milano 2007.

VISONÀ, G. (ed.), *Dialogo con Trifone*, Edizioni Paoline, Milano 1988.

VISONÀ, G. (ed.), *Didachè, insegnamento degli apostoli*, Edizioni Paoline, Milano 2000.

VOCI, A., *Processi psicosociali nei gruppi*, Editori Laterza, Bari 2003.

Acknowledgements

For the encouragement to publish this book and for all the practical help received in translating and reviewing it, my gratitude goes to Juli Howe, Massimo Lucci and Simone Frattini.

Index

Foreword..3

Introduction 9

   The dispute over paedobaptism 9

   Historical overview 13

Chapter I 18

   Didache...18

   Letter of Barnabas 23

   Shepherd of Hermas 29

Chapter II 37

   Apology of Aristides of Athens..............................37

   Apologies of Justin Martyr....................................44

Chapter III 59

   Against Heresies by Irenaeus of Lyons 59

   The transition to paedobaptism..............................65

   On baptism by Tertullian......................................70

   Apostolic Tradition...78

Conclusion...83

Postface 91

Abbreviations 94

Bibliography..95

Acknowledgements 98

www.ingramcontent.com/pod-product-compliance
Lightning Source LLC
Chambersburg PA
CBHW021139260726
48656CB00023B/675